To Rose —

The Best is yet
To Come!
God Bless You!
Dr. Willie Jolley

Advance Praise for
Turn Setbacks into Greenbacks

"Willie Jolley has written another incredible self-empowerment guide that will enable you to 'snatch victory from the jaws of defeat.' This powerful, timely survival manual will expand your vision and teach you how to succeed where others are failing. It will help you to develop the mind-set and skill set to convert setbacks into cash."

—Les Brown, best-selling author, award-winning speaker, and television and radio personality

"This book is full of change and challenge, pride and power, significance and success. Willie Jolley is an emotional power source whose energy is just barely contained in this wonderful book. When you open it, you'll feel the vitality of unrealized choices, and when you close it, you'll feel energized to change your life for your own benefit and for those around you."

—Alan Weiss, PhD, author of *Million Dollar Consulting* and *Thrive!*

"In this book, Willie Jolley hits a home run on the topic of personal and professional success and wealth building! Read it and then re-read it . . .

and then tell everyone you know to get a copy and read it! That way everyone you know will grow their wealth!"

—Larry Winget, television personality and best-selling author of *You're Broke Because You Want to Be* and *Your Kids Are Your Own Fault*

"Willie Jolley is committed to developing wealth in people around the world, and this book is a true example of that commitment! Read it, and you will be inspired and empowered to grow your success and your wealth!"

—Kelvin Boston, host of the *Moneywise* series on PBS, and author of *Who's Afraid to Be A Millionaire?*

"Willie Jolley has written a book, *Turn Setbacks into Greenbacks*, that will empower and inspire you to greater success and achievement! I highly recommend reading this book!"

—Wally Amos, best-selling author, speaker, positive thinker, and founder, Chip & Cookie

TURN
SETBACKS
INTO
GREENBACKS

TURN
SETBACKS
INTO
GREENBACKS

7 Secrets for Going Up in Down Times

WILLIE JOLLEY

John Wiley & Sons, Inc.

Published by John Wiley & Sons, Inc., Hoboken, New Jersey.
Published simultaneously in Canada.

For general information on our other products and services or for technical
support, please contact our Customer Care Department within the United
States at (800) 762-2974, outside the United States at (317) 572-3993 or via
fax (317) 572-4002.

Wiley also publishes its books in a variety of electronic formats. Some content that
appears in print may not be available in electronic books. For more information
about Wiley products, visit our Web site at www.wiley.com.

Library of Congress Cataloging-in-Publication Data:

Jolley, Willie.
    Turn setbacks into greenbacks : 7 secrets for going up in down times / by Willie
Jolley.
       p. cm.
    ISBN 978-0-470-55472-2 (cloth)
    1.   Success in business–Psychological aspects. 2.   Success. 3.   Recessions.
    I. Title.
    HF5386.J76 2010
    658.4'09–dc22   2009038779

Printed in the United States of America

10 9 8 7 6 5 4 3 2 1

*I dedicate this book to my children Latoya and
William. And to my brother's children,
Victor, Vincent, Rashida, Vivian,
Christina, Noble, Jr., and Nathan,
who became my children when their father
(my brother) passed away.*

*I have done my best to teach each of
you wealth-building principles.
I pray you use them and make a point
to share them with generations to come!*

*I also dedicate this book to my family members who
have made their transition since my last book.
To my mother, Catherine B. Jolley, my brother,
Noble Jolley, Sr., my father-in-law,
Rev. Rivers S. Taylor, Sr., and my Aunt
Eunice Ragland . . . I say this privately
and publicly, "I could curse because
you are gone, but I choose to celebrate
that you came this way!
I will always love you!"*

Contents

Foreword   Terry Paulson   *xi*

Acknowledgments   *xvii*

Prologue   *xix*

Preface   *xxi*

*Introduction: The Secrets to Turning
Setbacks into Comebacks*   *xxxv*

1   **Make Up Your Mind . . .
    Get Pressed, But Do Not Panic!**   **1**

2   **Don't Willingly Participate or
    Commiserate**   **43**

3   **Don't Let Your Pride Poison
    Your Prosperity**   **59**

4   **Don't Stop Thinking and Dreaming
    about the Power and Possibilities
    of Tomorrow**   **69**

5   **Be Proactive**   **95**

6   **Be Creative**   **129**

7   **Be Prayerful**   **147**

Conclusion   *161*

About the Author   *165*

Foreword

> I don't believe in a law to prevent a man from getting rich; it would do more harm than good. So while we do not propose any war on capital, we do wish to allow the humblest man an equal chance to get rich with everybody else.
>
> —*Abraham Lincoln*

L incoln understood what many do not. In a creative, free enterprise society like the United States, many aspiring and motivated citizens can still work hard to make money, save their money, then to invest, and ultimately to become entrepreneurs or owners of capital to create their own wealth.

The American Dream is alive and well. You have every right, even a responsibility, to live your dream. Those who say that we're in a time when there are no opportunities just don't know where to look.

Help is on the way, and you are holding it right now. Willie Jolley's timely and informative book, *Turn Setbacks into Greenbacks*, appeals to your best hopes, not your worst fears, to your confidence, rather than your doubts. Finally, a book that puts the focus where it belongs—what you can do now to ensure your own economic future by putting the insights and strategies provided into action.

Sound too good to be true? It's not! In this age of constant change and continuing economic uncertainty, waiting for someone else to hand you the lifestyle and success you want is just wishful thinking. Forget waiting for the Tooth Fairy, the Fairy Godmother, or Washington politicians to make you wealthy! Get rid of any thought of victim thinking—the obstacles you face and the answers you seek don't come from others. You have what it takes to be a resilient and optimistic achiever.

Optimism isn't developed through just repeating positive thinking mantras about how great life is . . . without any precipitating action. You can start with the positive thinking, but then you must take positive action! This book isn't motivational hype; it is filled with step-by-step action to move you from where you are to where you want to be. Research shows that optimism is earned through a track record of overcoming obstacles. The more obstacles you overcome, the more you believe that you can overcome

Foreword

the next one. Optimists are realists. They want to know the problems they face, because they believe they can overcome or get around them to become successful. This book won't give you wealth; you'll have to earn it one day, one choice, one action at a time.

This information-rich book provides a proven road map. You will learn the financial skills, the plan, and attitudes you need to achieve your own American Dream. You'll learn how to keep hope alive in this age of cynicism by trading feelings of helplessness and frustration for resilience, resourcefulness, and persistence, as you turn adversity and obstacles into financial opportunities.

The only person you even remotely control is yourself; so get busy investing your worry time in a constructive action plan one day at a time. Every successful entrepreneur will tell you that the journey to wealth is filled with closed doors, setbacks, failures, and the satisfying joy of achieving success along the way. Don't let anyone call you a victim; you are a resilient achiever who is choosing to live your dream. Wealth should not be your primary goal; it is the byproduct of transforming your gifts and innovate ideas into a mission that makes a difference people are willing to pay for. When you find your gifts, identify your mission, focus your efforts, and claim a positive attitude, wealth and meaning are around the corner!

I've seen Willie Jolley in action as a speaker and inspiring motivator. His advice and common-sense insights are as enlivening as they are empowering. He's been where you've been, and he's taken his own journey to success after success. Now, he's ready to give you the lessons learned along the way.

Willie Jolley not only informs and energizes; he communicates in ways that people can understand and appreciate. His book highlights some *keepers* that I can't wait to use:

The bad times have come and will pass; they came to pass . . . not to stay!

Leave victim thinking to others—if 10 percent are unemployed, 90 percent are working. Be one of the victors, not one of the victims.

Don't do what's comfortable—do what's necessary.

Be proactive—Get up and get going!

Success won't come to you—sell and market by talking to people about your business, your prod-ucts, and your services.

When you pray, move your feet so God has something to work with!

All it takes for the American Dream to work its magic for you is to claim it for yourself. Do something better that costs less. Create the better mousetrap, and make it more affordable, and people will beat a path to your door to buy it!

Innovate and make a move. If early attempts fail, get up and make new choices . . . and succeed. How do you start? If you are not sure what to do first, start by getting up and doing something really simple . . . read this book! By the way, when you finally do succeed, be ready to write to Willie about what worked for you in making your dream live. He just may use your story on a motivational minute message. You may even read about yourself in his next book.

So, devour Willie Jolley's *Turn Setbacks into Greenbacks* and get busy turning your worries into profitable opportunities, one day at a time. Don't just read it once; reread the parts that fit you . . . and then share the insights learned from this book with others. Tell your network about this book and let them know that whatever they are experiencing is nothing but a setup for their greater comeback, and these principles can help them to turn those setbacks into greenbacks. Finally, give the author the greatest compliment by putting the insights into action to help turn your life around! Remember, delivering on your economic dreams is both your opportunity and your responsibility.

—Terry Paulson, PhD, professional speaker, national columnist, and author of *The Optimism Advantage: 50 Simple Truths to Transform Your Attitudes and Actions into Results*

Acknowledgments

I want to thank my wife, Dee Taylor-Jolley, for her continuous support and inspiration. I want to thank my children, William and LaToya, for their input in this project. I want to thank my marketing manager, Cheryl Ragin, for her help in getting this book finalized and ready for print. I want to thank the members of my Mastermind Group, Bill Cates, Steven Gaffney, Zemira Jones, and Suzi Pomerantz, for their advice and input as I started throwing around the concept of the book. I want to thank all of my speaker buddies at the National Speakers Association who are always so willing to share ideas and insights. I want to thank all the guests on my XM Radio show who shared their wealth of information and advice on success and achievement. I want to give a special thanks to my dear friend Sam Horn (www.samhorn.com), who is a genius when it comes to putting literary ideas into a catchy concept. As I started to work on the concept of helping people create wealth even in the midst of a recession, I struggled with how to give it a succinct title. I was considering a few titles, including: *How to Turn Economic Setbacks into Comebacks, How to Go Up in Down Economic Times, How to Get through the Recession and Get Rich,* and a few others. During that time, I attended a networking dinner Sam gave for some of her friends, and I mentioned my ideas. She said, "Willie, your book *A Setback Is a Setup for a Comeback* has created a new catchphrase that many people around the world have made a common part of their vernacular. You are now well-known as the Comeback Guru, because of the book and your PBS special, *Turning Setbacks into Comebacks,* but it sounds like you now want to talk about creating a financial comeback, and so you are talking about focusing on the greenbacks!" I said, "Sam, you are absolutely right!" I want to thank Sam Horn for her genius and her willingness to share it. Finally, I want to thank my Pastor and friend, John K. Jenkins Pastor of The First Bapist Church of Glenarden, Maryland, and all the people around the world who have continued to encourage me and pray for me and my family. I give God the glory for all my friends and prayer partners around the world! God Bless You!

Prologue

If you have had financial challenges—lost your job, your home, or your savings—and if this makes you think that you are about to lose your mind, then this book can help! And if you have not had any challenges with money, I definitely recommend you read this book, because if you live long enough, you will eventually have some economic setbacks.

I want to say that this book is about money! Money plays a major part in our daily activities, from what we eat to where we sleep and the level of comfort we have in our lives. Money is important. Some say that money makes the world go round; I say that *money matters!* And since money matters, we might as well talk about it and help people develop a healthy perspective on money and how to increase their prosperity, even in tough economic times. We need to talk about wealth and why it is important to not only turn our setbacks into comebacks but also turn our setbacks into greenbacks!

Preface

"Money, money, money, money . . . Money!"
Those are the lyrics from the hit song "For
the Love of Money," by the O'Jays. The song was a
massive hit for them in the 1970s, and it is still
popular today. In fact it was the song chosen as the
opening theme for the popular show *The Apprentice*, with Donald Trump, in which contestants
competed to work for Donald in the hopes of
making a lot of—you guessed it—money. Let's
face it, money is a popular topic in popular music
and in mass media, with shows like *Fast Money*,
Mad Money, Who Wants to be a Millionaire?, and
Who Wants to Marry a Millionaire? There are
entire magazines and newspapers dedicated to
money—making it, saving it, investing it—you
name it. Money is a major part of our culture.

Yet we have all heard the saying, "Money isn't
everything!" To that, I want to say I agree, money is
not everything, *but* . . . money certainly is an
important thing—a VERY important thing! When

times get tough, money's role as a necessary part of our lives becomes even clearer. Money is important, and so we must talk about it and develop skills to generate money and manage the money we generate.

Is It Really Necessary to Talk about Money?

Occasionally over the years I have one person or another come up to me after a speech and ask why must I talk about money. They say life is about more than money. My answer to this is always the same: I could not agree more! Life is about so much more than money.

I have said it in earlier books, and I will say it again now: Money is important, but it is not everything. Money is a powerful motivational tool, yet it is not the most powerful tool. I believe money is a powerful motivator, but love is much more powerful. I ask you to stop and think for a moment, and go with me through this scenario.

Assume a person came up to you and offered you $1,000 to walk on a board that is 500 feet long and 2 feet wide. The board is laid on the ground, and all you have to do is walk down the board from one end to the other. Would you walk the board for $1,000? I hope you say yes, because that would be an easy $1,000. Now let's say that the person laid that same board across the roofs of two matching skyscrapers and asked you to walk along the board from one skyscraper to the other, without a net below you. Would you still walk the board from end to end for $1,000? Most people I ask say, "No!"

Now stop and think a moment about someone you love, maybe a parent, or your child, or your brother or sister or your best friend. Imagine that the person who wanted you to walk on the board was holding your loved one halfway across the board between the two skyscrapers, and the person told you that if you didn't walk the board, then they would throw your loved one off the board. Would you be willing to walk the board now? Most people I have asked say "Yes! Without a doubt!" When all is said and done, people will do more for love than they will do for money. Money is important, but it is not everything.

Life is about family and friends and faith, but when we are short of money, then money becomes a pressing concern on our minds. For most of the time, we feel that money is important but does not really take all of our focus. But when we get to a place where we don't have any money, then it becomes a big thing and the predominant issue that preoccupies our thinking.

I have noticed that the people who usually say that money is not important are the ones who have some money, or at least know where their next meal is coming from. But if you don't have money for food and you have fears about where you will sleep, money tends to be a greater issue. I typically get the response about money not being important from one or two people out of 100. The other 98 percent of the people I talk to after my speeches are either looking for ways to increase their income so they either help their families live better lives or are committed to leaving a legacy, so they are looking for ways to make more money so they can give more money.

I want to say right up front that in this book I will talk about money, and how you can get more money. I want to talk about the fact that money is an important and necessary part of our society. Some people feel that money is not important and not good to talk about in public conversation. Others feel that money is bad and is the "root of all evil," yet the Scripture actually states that it is "the love of money" that is the root of all evil. It is when money becomes your god that it becomes a terrible master. Having money is usually not the problem, but it is a problem when money has you!

If the love of money is the root of all evil, then lack of money is what causes the evil tree to sprout and grow. In tough economic times, we can actually see how money—and the lack of it—can cause people great amounts of anxiety and grief and can make them do terrible things. When money becomes tight, it touches every household and segment of society. No one is immune to the sting of the economic pinch. When people have no money, or are afraid to spend the money they have, it can bring economies and countries to their knees. During the tough times, the wolves', tails fall out, revealing the wolves who are hidden in sheep's clothing during the good times. Bernie Madoff is a perfect example of a wolf in sheep's clothing. He "made off" with the life savings of thousands of hardworking people who had invested everything they had with him. As we all know now, he was running the biggest Ponzi scheme in history.

During tough times, people become frightened and stop spending money. When people stop spending money on items like homes and cars, that has an impact on the workers who make and sell homes and cars, and those people have less money to spend on the regular items of necessity. And the cycle continues so that it eventually affects everyone. The lack of money can have an overwhelming impact on a society. Money is not everything, but it is very important to life. As Rita Davenport says, "Money is not everything . . . but it is right up there with breathing!"

Why Is It Important to Be Wealthy?

Money can't buy happiness, but neither can poverty.

—Leo Rosten

I ask why it is important to develop personal wealth because, deep down, most people ask themselves how they can make more money, but only a few move beyond the question to take action. If I asked the question, "Who wants to be a millionaire?" most people would say "I do!" The people who answered "I want to become a millionaire" really would like to become millionaires, but very few actually make it happen, because to them, wealth is about luxurious living and extravagance, not about practical day-to-day existence. In contrast, I say that wealth is not about extravagance and living in the lap of luxury but rather about living the kind of life that offers you and your loved ones the best opportunities for health and longevity. Most people want to be wealthy, but very few have decided that it is *important* to be wealthy. I say that it is important to be wealthy! Why? Because money gives you options.

Money gives you options for many important aspects of life including housing, health care, and education. As I have traveled around the country speaking, I often meet people who say they want more money, yet have not made the decision to take the necessary actions to create additional income. These people do not understand that money creates longevity, because the lack of money has a negative impact on your peace of mind and your stress level. Statistics show that poor people tend to have shorter life spans because of stress and the lack of preventive health programs, exercise programs, and adequate health care. Money gives you options.

Some years ago, I heard a story about a young boy who developed a strange growth on his leg. His mom took him to her health-care organization, where the doctor examined the young boy and said that he had a rare illness. His recommendation was to amputate the boy's leg at the knee.

The mother was stunned and told the doctor that the young boy was a very talented soccer player, and she wondered what other options were available. When the doctor replied that amputation was the most efficient way of handling the illness, the mother asked if she could get a second opinion, and she was directed down the hall to another doctor.

The second doctor looked at the chart and came to the same conclusion, that amputation at the knee was the most efficient way of handling the situation. The mother again proclaimed that the young boy was a gifted athlete and loved running and playing sports, and she hoped that maybe there were other options besides amputation. The doctor shrugged and said "Sorry, but that is the most efficient way to handle the situation."

The mother then began to research and found that although the illness was serious, it was not life threatening and also found that there could be options other than amputation. She approached her health-care organization again to get another opinion on the matter, but was told that her plan only allowed two opinions on the same item. She told the lady on the phone, "I appreciate your candor, but I have a little money in the bank, so I will check out some other options on my own!"

The mother went on the Internet and found a specialist in Baltimore, Maryland. She contacted his office and got an appointment. He was not a participant in her health-care plan, so she had to pay for the visit out of pocket. She reminded herself, "I have some money so I will pay for the visit." She and her son flew to Baltimore and the specialist spent a considerable amount of time with the young boy. Finally he finished the exam and said, "I am sure you were told that amputation was the best way to handle this problem, but I don't agree. It is the most efficient and cost-effective way to handle the problem, but it is not the only way or the best way to handle the problem." He continued, "I can save your son's leg. It will not be cheap, but I can save his leg." The mother looked at the doctor and said, "I have some money in the bank; you do what you have to do to save my baby's leg!" The doctor went on to perform the treatment, and save the young boy's leg. This example is just one example that, yes, although money is not everything, it does give you options.

Sometimes tough economic situations have nothing to do with the world's economy but have to do with your personal economy. In other words, there might be times when the economy is healthy, but you have hit a personal financial bump in the road and are in need of a personal economic recovery. Either way, whether you have lots of money or you are experiencing a lack of money, these situations can play a major part in your stress levels and in your health and wellness.

This raises a rather interesting question: How do we handle the anxieties that appear when we realize that we have a lack of money? The answer is further in this book . . . along with advice for not only surviving tough economic conditions, but thriving. That's right, *thriving*! I will take you on a journey that demonstrates how to handle economic downturns, both financially and mentally, and shows what it will take for you to face your financial fears and win in spite of the economic situation you are facing. It will help you to get a winner's attitude about wealth.

I mentioned dealing with money and our attitude to money because our attitude has a big impact on how we handle money, especially in tough times. It doesn't even take a full-on depression for people to get depressed and overwhelmed by the gloom and doom of tough economic times. However, we can turn an economic setback into an advantage and position ourselves for super success and wealth. This is the time for *you* to become wealthy!

Depressions, recessions, economic downturns, or simply being broke and having more month than you have money—it all leads back to the same place: WE NEED MONEY! Money is important, and most people not only need money, they need a lot more money—and if they have children, they especially need lots of money!

There was a time in my life when I would have said, "Money is not important, it's the love of friends and family that is really important!" I have learned over the years that I was half right. Ultimately, the love of friends and family is the most important. We all know that when we come to our last days, we will not think about the money we have but the love of friends and family. But without money, that last day may come much earlier than it should. Having money does not guarantee long life, but statistics clearly show that people with money tend to live longer than those without money.

In my earlier books, I talked about the importance of friends and family and how you must nurture those relationships, because when all is said and done, they will be the most important parts of your life. I still believe that is true, but money must be on your list of important items or you will stress the seams of the relationships. Statistics show that divorce and marital strife increase in tough economic times. Money, or the lack thereof, can greatly affect the stress level in relationships. When tough times hit and you have children to feed and bills to pay, you come to the realization that money is very important. I have found that the tighter the economy gets, the more money becomes a focus. So let's deal with it, learn how to get through the tough times, and get on the road to wealth.

As mentioned earlier, the subject of money permeates our culture; we cannot escape it. Money is everywhere. It is in our literature and in our magazines. There is a magazine called *Money*, and many newspapers, such as *The Wall Street Journal*, focus on money and financial news. And even my favorite book, the best-selling book of all time, the Bible, speaks about money more than 2,300 times.

In Ecclesiastes 10:19, the translation by Peterson reads, "Laughter and bread go together, and wine gives sparkle to life. But it is money that makes the world go round!" According to Howard Dayton, the chief executive officer of Crown Financial Ministries, 15 percent of everything Jesus says is about money.

And in Deuteronomy 8:18 the Bible says, "And you shall remember the Lord your God, for it is He who gives you power to get wealth, that He may establish His covenant which He swore to your fathers, as it is this day!" That means that God gives us the power and ability to get wealth, yet the wealth must be to establish his covenant, which is to help others. I believe that God wants His children to be wealthy and He will help you to become wealthy, if you are willing to be a good steward of that wealth and show a pattern of using your wealth wisely.

My goal is to help you to create wealth and have more money. I want to help you create not only financial wealth, but also success in your personal and family relationships. I want to help you to turn your economic setbacks into exciting comebacks—in fact, to turn your setbacks into greenbacks!

Before we get into the meat of this book, I think it is important for me to share a little about myself. I am an inspirational/motivational speaker, singer, media personality, and author, and I have been blessed to write books and create programs that have become bestsellers around the world. For the last 20 years or so, I have made it my business to learn as much as I can about success and to share that knowledge with millions of people via speeches, books, radio, television, columns, music, the Internet, e-mail, and other forums—even a daily Willie Jolley Wake-Up Call. I have personally made millions of dollars and have had the opportunity to develop friendships with numerous millionaires and billionaires, and have learned incredible lessons from them about life and success. I also want you to know that as much as this book is about finances and building wealth, that information is secondary. The primary thing that I will share in this book is how you will personally grow, and how this growth will manifest itself as financial success.

I want to state emphatically that I am grateful to be born in America and experience the opportunities available in this country. I am grateful that I can live in a time when I can talk about my faith, my family, and my thoughts about money openly. I can state emphatically that I am pro-God, pro-family, and pro–free enterprise!

I thank God for life and for the great blessings He has given me. Of all the things I am grateful for, the most important thing to me, besides my faith, is my family. As we juggle our many responsibilities in life, we must make sure to take extra special care of the family ball, because that is the one made of glass, while the others are made of rubber. If you drop the other balls, they will bounce, but if you drop the family ball it may very well shatter, and in many cases, it cannot be put back together again. So I recommend you take special care of the family ball, because it is precious and very fragile.

Finally, I am in favor of free enterprise. I believe we live in a time and a place where all things truly are possible, and that the level of our thinking ultimately determines the level of our impact and our income! So I recommend you dream big, think big, do big, and reap the benefits in a big way!

Now that you know where I stand, you can understand what I will say and why I will say it, and you can take the information that follows and craft a greater existence and a better life! So let's get it on! Let's *go big*! Let's turn these setbacks into GREENBACKS!

Introduction:
The Secrets to Turning
Setbacks into Comebacks

We will all have setbacks in life—not maybe, not might, but for sure. Before we talk about how to turn setbacks into greenbacks, I think we need to review the basics of turning setbacks into comebacks. In my book, *A Setback Is a Setup for a Comeback*, I interviewed people who had incredible setbacks and were able to turn them into amazing comebacks. Some of the people I wrote about were famous, like Lee Iacocca, Wally Famous Amos, and Tina Turner. But what about the people who might not be famous? Would these principles work for them as well? The answer was a resounding "Yes!" In fact, the stories that inspired me the most were the stories of everyday people who had setbacks and turned them into great comebacks.

Like the young man I interviewed who had a small business and two small children and was struggling to provide for his family. He had a setback with his business and went bankrupt. He lost his house and ended up living on the street, but that was not the end of his story. He came back! And his comeback was incredible. He went on to build a company called Damark, one of the largest merchandising companies in America.

Or how about a lady I interviewed, Mrs. Doris DeBoe, a ninth-grade math teacher who was diagnosed with cancer and given only a few months to live. She was stunned when she got the diagnosis but made up her mind that she was not going to die. She looked the doctors in their eyes and said, "I am not going to die any time soon. I am going to live for 25 more years because I have too many children to teach!" I am glad to say I was able to celebrate her eighty-third birthday with her, and when she passed in 2009, she did not die from cancer (she beat cancer four times), instead she died from old age. I spoke at her funeral and we celebrated her life and how she accomplished her goal to beat cancer. She lived for more than 25 years after the doctors had given her six months. In my book, *A Setback Is a Setup for a Comeback,* I share a powerful quote from Mrs. DeBoe. She said, "Tell the people in your book that I might have cancer, but cancer does not have me! Also tell them that doctors can give you the diagnosis, but God always gives the prognosis!"

I also interviewed a woman who was moving up the corporate ladder, but just before reaching the top, she was fired due to her age. After giving so much to the company, she was devastated when they let her go. Yet, she didn't give up. She kept fighting—and eventually she came back . . . and bought the company!

Throughout the book, I shared story after story of people who had setbacks and turned them into comebacks. And I learned that there was a common thread that was apparent in all the stories. There were four common elements: the power of vision, the power of decision, the power of action, and the power of desire.

1. Focus Your Vision

Where there is no vision, the people perish . . .

—*Proverbs 29:18*

Where you put your focus and your energy will determine where you will go. If you focus on the setback and the challenges it brought you, you cannot effectively move forward. However, when you focus your vision on what you want to become—despite the setback—then you're using the setback for what it really is: a transition period.

Since we will all go through some sort of change or setback at one time or another, it's important to be able to look past the obstacle and plan your future strategies. To develop your new focus, ask yourself these questions:

- What is the big picture I have for my future?
- What can I do differently to keep this setback from occurring again?
- What goals do I want to achieve in the next three, six, and twelve months?
- How can I use this setback as a learning experience?

Use the answers to these questions as your guide to develop your new focus.

2. Make a Decision

Both success and failure are decisions. Once your vision is in place, you need to decide you're going to win despite the setback. The truth is that successful people choose to be successful. They understand that success is a choice, not a chance. They understand that decisions and choices are integral parts of the success formula. No matter what setback they encounter, they decide to overcome it and prevail.

Decisions you'll have to make to overcome a setback include:

- *Who are my advisers?* Negative advisers who focus on the setback won't help you overcome it. You need to decide to associate with positive people who share your vision.
- *Is my new goal big enough?* Just because you had a setback doesn't mean you have to start over small. Make a decision to see the big picture first. Then you can work your way backward to meeting that goal.
- *What steps must I take to meet my goal?* Plan out and decide specifically what you will do to meet your new goal. For example, if your goal is to increase sales by 33 percent, write out what you will do to accomplish that and the timeframe you're allowing yourself to meet the goal.

3. Take Action

A decision without action is simply an illusion, and an action without a vision is mere confusion. Yet a vision plus decisive action can change the world.

Once you decide on the various factors that will go into making your new vision a reality, you must take action on each and every one. Unfortunately, many people never act on their decisions. While they have every intention of making their new vision a reality, they lack the determination and persistence that are required in order to take action.

By acting on a decision, you're also taking responsibility for the setback. The word *decision* is taken from the Greek word for "to cut." When you make an *in*cision, you cut "in," and when you make a *de*cision, you cut "off!" Take responsibility and cut off those people, places, and things that will keep you from living your dreams. Once you take responsibility for your actions, you're ready to move forward and attain your next goal. Remember, you might not be responsible for getting knocked down, but you are responsible for getting back up. Only those who act achieve their goals.

4. Keep the Desire

Desire is the degree of energy you're willing to exert to reach your goal. In other words, how badly do you want not only to survive but thrive, and what are you willing to do to achieve success?

Imagine I took you to Giants Stadium and told you that somewhere on that football field,

$1 million was buried—and then I offered you a shovel. Would you be interested in digging for the million dollars? Most people would say, "Yes!" I believe that even though you wouldn't have the first clue on where to start digging or how deep to go, most people would be willing to dig and dig and dig for that $1 million. In fact, on television reality shows, we see lots of people who eat worms and take part in other antics for a chance at a jackpot, so I have to imagine that digging up a football field isn't so bad! The point is that you are willing to go out and dig with the anticipation that there will be a reward for your efforts. You must have the determination to dig and keep fighting for your dreams. You must be determined and persistent to achieve your goals. I believe the same is true for life! There are millions of dollars out in the world with your name on them, waiting for you . . . but to get the money, you must be determined and persistent—and you must keep digging!

Many people who take action quickly give up because their desire falters. Either a new idea strikes them and they lose focus, or they encounter another minor setback and become discouraged. To reach the new goal you have set for yourself, you must have the desire to consistently follow through with every action, even if it involves a degree of risk. While taking a risk may be intimidating, especially after a setback, it's a necessary ingredient to reaching your new goal. Turning your setback into a comeback will take initiative and action. And initiative and action always involve risk: no guts, no glory—no risk, no reward! Progress always involves risk. You cannot get to second base if you are afraid to leave first.

Decide how badly you want to achieve the goal, and then keep going after it until you achieve it. Remember, a setback is not an *if* proposition; it's a *when* proposition. And when one occurs in your life, you need to make a conscious decision to view it not as a problem but as a learning opportunity. You must decide what you're going to do about the setback and focus on the solution.

As I interviewed people for *A Setback Is a Setup for a Comeback*, I found that there was a consistent pattern—Vision, Decision, Action, and Desire—that ran through the stories they told me. I started doing more research on simple steps that could be implemented in our everyday activities to turn our setbacks into comebacks, and I identified a 12-step program for turning your setbacks into comebacks! The 12 steps are:

1. *Check your perspective.* What you see is what you get! It is not so much that seeing is

believing, but rather that believing is the key to eventually seeing!

2. *Recognize it's life.* Life 101 says, "Some days you're the windshield, and some days you're the bug!" Life happens—setbacks happen to everyone, but it is your attitude that will eventually make the difference.

3. *Focus on your goal.* If the dream is big enough the problems don't matter. The bigger the dream, the bigger the reward.

4. *Make the tough decisions.* Now that you have had a setback, what are you going to do about it? It is not so much what happens to you but what you do about it that counts!

5. *Decide to stay positive.* Positive people tend to live longer and tend to enjoy the journey much more!

6. *Stop and think.* Step back, look in, check out, and think up! Look at all your options. You always have options but the key to success is to make wise choices.

7. *Take action.* You can have lights and cameras but nothing happens until you take action! Many talk about living their dreams, but only those who act on their dreams are able to make them into realities.

8. *Take responsibility.* Face it, trace it, erase it, and replace it. First, face the problem. Then,

trace the problem and learn from it, erase the problem—don't dwell on it. Finally, replace the problem—replace the negative in your life with something positive and inspiring.

9. *Harness your anger.* Use it for good! Anger is the word danger without the "d". The "d" is for discipline! Anger is a natural emotion—the key is to be disciplined.

10. *Have faith, and remind yourself that you are blessed and highly favored!* Positive, courageous faith can give you power for the toughest journeys.

11. *Affirm to win, refuse to lose, and never give up!* Never, ever, ever, give up! Winners never quit and quitters never win!

12. *Have an attitude of gratitude!* Learn to find the blessings in every burden. Be grateful for each and every day!

Every successful person has had setbacks; however, he or she realizes that a setback is not the end of the road, but rather a bend in the road . . . and the only ones who crash are those who fail to make the turn. When you view your setback as a chance for future growth, every challenge can have a positive outcome, and every personal setback can eventually be seen as nothing but a setup for an incredible comeback.

Are You Serious?

I got a note from an old friend from my time as a nightclub singer. He said he had seen me on television and wanted to know what I did to change my life. I told him that when I was fired from the nightclub, which I had built into one of the top nightclubs in Washington D.C., because it was more cost effective to buy a karaoke machine than pay a band, I decided to change . . . and as Jim Rohn says, "Once you change, everything changes for you!"

I told him I made a commitment to grow and to expand my thinking. I started a course of self-development and made a commitment to read books with a positive message, listen to motivational tapes, and attend lots of motivational seminars and rallies. In short, I told him that I decided to get serious about my success. I made up my mind that I was going to do whatever was necessary to develop myself and grow into a person who was ready for success. I remember Les Brown telling me once that most people are "seriously, not serious about success." He said they talk about it, and talk about it, and talk about it, but never do anything about it. So I made up my mind to get serious!

I made a commitment to get up early and stay up late; I made a commitment to read everything I could about self development. I turned off the television and heavily invested my time in books and audios. I made the commitment to get on the phone and make sales calls. I would get on the phone early in the morning and would continue until late into the evening, and when I got tired and wanted to stop, I would always make one more call. I made a commitment that on a daily basis I would do more than I was paid to do, and give more than I was expected to give, and go further than I was asked to go. And I have found it to be true that if you do more than you are paid to do, then one day you will be paid more for what you do. And if you do the things today that others won't do, you will have the things tomorrow that others won't have.

My old friend then asked me what three things I do on a daily basis. I told him that I start each day the same way, with prayer and meditation. I thank God for each morning as I get out of bed and I proudly proclaim, "This is the day that the Lord has made, and I am glad and rejoice in it!" I have an attitude of gratitude, because I have another opportunity to go out and live my dream!

Second, I ask myself, *Willie, what would you do today if you were serious?* Once I get the answers, I write them down and get to work on making my dreams into realities. Then I ask myself, *What can you do today to get better?* I have learned that success is the result of personal and professional development and that getting better requires daily development. Greatness at any task does not happen in a day, but rather day by day. It is the daily regimen that makes the difference. Just like you grow your muscles little by little, so, too, do you grow yourself and your success little by little, day by day.

I told my friend that this was not rocket science, but it did take a PhD—Persistence, Hunger, and Determination! Most of all, it takes a commitment to grow ourselves so we can grow our futures. Then we must make a commitment to that commitment! So I will ask you now and ask you again over and over again. . . . *Are you serious?*

The question that constantly is asked during tough times is, "How in the world do we survive this ordeal?" There are no easy answers, but there are concepts that have been time-tested and solutions that work. These concepts worked in the 1930s and have worked throughout the other recessions we have seen; they will work today, as well. In fact, we have seen many of the same tendencies today that were seen in years past. Historically, movie studios have seen the highest ticket sales in the midst of tough economic times, and companies that specialize in home theater and home entertainment see incredible increases in sales during tough times. It is in tough times when we can build great wealth. Yet these principles only work if you are willing to work them, and you are willing to diligently apply them to your life.

Warren Buffett, one of the wealthiest men in the world, said that this is a challenging time, yet it's also a great time to create wealth. He said that recessions and economic downturns are historic—they have come before and will probably come again in our lifetimes. He also said we should learn from history. We have seen worse economic situations, and each one ended with the economy being better than it had been before. He said with each recovery, the best days are truly ahead for those who are willing to think differently and not buy into negative commentaries and negative outlooks. Buffett feels that an economic downturn offers great opportunities to those who have a positive outlook and have made up their mind not to follow the crowd of negative thinkers.

In an interview on CNBC, Buffett said, "The bad news creates fear and anxiety, but you must fight the fear and realize that everything will be alright in time. The free enterprise system works! Occasionally the machine gets gummed up, but it will right itself and you can trust that the system works!" According to the *Wall Street Journal*, after Buffett spoke on the subject of banking and savings, saying that the best days were ahead for the banking industry, the stock prices for Well Fargo bank rose more than 24 percent!

Buffett also advised his listeners to look to the future with optimism and excitement, and look for the opportunities that are all around. Finally, he said, "When other people were greedy (during the Internet boom and eventual bust), that was when I laid back! But when the others were fearful, then that was when I was greedy!"

I agree with Warren Buffett: A time of economic downturn is when we should examine the patterns that existed in the past, while looking optimistically to the future. It is the time to look for opportunities and look at possibilities and be bold. Those who think differently and open their eyes to the opportunities and possibilities are those who will prosper. Jack Adgate of The HON Company wrote, "What does every recession have in common? They all ended with very different results for businesses. At the end of the 1990 recession, Wal-Mart had pulled ahead of Sears, Gillette beat Colgate-Palmolive, and Merrill Lynch beat Bear Stearns."

The main question is whether you see a setback (such as a recession) as a problem or as a strategic opportunity. What do you want your life and business to look like once you've overcome the setback?

In changing and challenging times, I believe it is necessary to think differently! If you are willing to do different things and do some of the old things differently, you will be able to go beyond surviving and get to a place of thriving. And you will be able to consistently turn your economic setbacks into greenbacks!

The Road Less Traveled

As we grow older, we live through one challenging experience after another. As M. Scott Peck stated in the first line of his book, *The Road Less Traveled*, "Life is difficult." Period! He's right; life is difficult. Life is challenging. And there are times when life is downright unfair. Yet life is still worth living. Even with the challenges and the difficulties we all must endure, life still is a beautiful thing! I have a sign on my desk that states, "Life does not have to be perfect to be wonderful!"

We all have some tough times and will eventually have some setbacks in our lives, yet there are great opportunities in the midst of the challenges. We will have some times of crisis, but we must understand the true definition of *crisis* to see the possibilities for our futures.

We typically think of crisis as a calamity, a time of hurt, pain, and despair. Yes, during tough times, there are hurt, pain, and despair, but that is not the totality of the situation. The word *crisis* is an interesting word because it has dual attributes: great challenge and difficulty, yet at the same time great opportunity! Napoleon Hill stated in his book *Think and Grow Rich*, "In every adversity there is always the seed for equal or greater benefit." In that spirit, let me share a few ideas that I believe will help you to get through any crisis and come out on the other side greater and better than you began!

As we get into the specific steps of this economic comeback, my goal is to give you specific strategies on how to not only survive, but to thrive, through this challenging time.

Warren Buffett was right: Now is the time! It is setbacks-into-greenbacks time! We will get through this! Get ready for your incredible comeback! Let's make it happen!

And now, on to the seven steps for turning setbacks into greenbacks!

TURN
SETBACKS
INTO
GREENBACKS!

Make Up Your Mind . . . Get Pressed, but Do Not Panic (Because Pressure Makes Diamonds, but Panic Makes Disasters)

> Tough times don't last but tough people do!
>
> —*Dr. Robert H Schuller*

Challenges with money happen to everyone at some time or another. I know it's not fun. In fact, I know it's quite the opposite—it's painful. When we experience an economic setback, whether personally or on a grander scale (like a recession or a depression), that feeling of losing control can shake our equilibrium, a feeling that none of us likes. Often, that lack of control is accompanied by an increased level of pressure and anxiety. When you're broke, it's hard to concentrate and see a future where money isn't short and paying bills isn't so difficult. The pressure gets stronger when money gets funny, and change gets strange! Yet the good news—the really good news—is that there is a solution to this problem, and it starts with your thinking!

First and Foremost, Make Up Your Mind

I have been through the pressure of tough economic times before, and I learned some valuable lessons in the process. I learned that pressure actually can make diamonds in your life, but it is critical that when the pressure comes your way, you make up your mind to use the pressure to make you stronger and better, not make you weaker and bitter. Start thinking differently. Think positively and concentrate on what you want, rather than what you don't want and what you fear. Why? Because whatever you focus on longest becomes the strongest!

Developing a winning mind-set is crucial. Make up your mind that you will win, somehow, some way, and that when the dust clears you will still be standing. It is like the movie *The Color Purple,* when Miss Celie decides to leave her mean, abusive husband, Mister. When she tells him she is going to leave, he begins to tell her that no one wants her, that she is ugly, and that she has never done anything of any worth. She looks at him with steely confidence and says, "I might be ugly, and I might not have done anything of any worth in your eyes . . . but I'm still here! I'm still here!" It was a declaration of achievement and a statement of worth! So, the first step to turning a setback into greenbacks is to make up your mind! To win in life and business, you must make up your mind— you must make the commitment that you are willing to go beyond your comfort zone. Once you make up your mind and make the commitment, you must be willing to keep working toward your goal until you reach it.

As with most things in life, the first step is always the most critical. Most people do not win in life, because they don't make up their minds and don't commit themselves to the goal. Goethe said, "Until one is committed there is hesitancy, the chance to draw back, always ineffectiveness. But the minute, the moment one definitely commits oneself, that is the moment that Providence (the hand of God) moves also. All manner of things occur that would never regularly have occurred. Boldness has magic and genius in it, begin it now!" If you want to get on the winner's track, the first step is to make up your mind, because nothing in life is more powerful than a made-up mind.

Most people have an "I hope I can" mind-set. But a person who has a made-up mind has an "I know I can! I know I will!" mind-set. These are the people who consistently seem to win in life and in business. They consistently beat the odds and continue to have success. They go through the tough economic times and come out on the other end better and wealthier. We know that stormy economic winds are going to blow, but if we have made up our minds that we are going to win, we find that we are on the right path to greater success.

Some years ago I was asked by Microsoft to initiate their new Web Meetings portal for the product kickoff program. While I was asked to head the Web Meetings portal, Donald Trump was asked to kick off the business development portal. As a result of this program, I was introduced to the Trump team. I had a chance to learn more about Donald Trump and his thinking, and why he continued to succeed even in challenging times. And one of the reasons for his consistent success is the way he thinks. I learned that Donald Trump thinks he will win even when all the odds are stacked against him. He has a made up mind and does not allow doubt or fear to creep into his thinking or limit his options.

Trump states that he faced repeated opposition when he first came to Manhattan to seek new projects to develop. It was a bad time for the real estate market in New York, and it was a bad economy, yet he made up his mind that this was really an opportunity. And as a result of his thinking, he was able to overcome the fear that kept others from acting during dire economic times. Most people were planning to wait until the economy turned around, but Trump decided that this was the time to move, and that he was going to be successful, come hell or high water. Once he made up his mind, he went to work on the challenges that faced him, and he eventually succeeded with that project. Since those early ventures, he has had one challenging project after another, and even had a time in the 1980s when the market went down and many of the banks called in their loans. But Trump again made up his mind. He decided to think outside the box and came up with a series of creative loan restructuring programs that would get everyone paid but would buy him time to get it done. He was able to succeed in those ventures as well, which led to more deals and more celebrity. Why? Because he made up his mind to win! I want you to make up your mind and get in the habit of going after success!

Once you make up your mind, you are halfway there—the battle is half-won. Very little actually happens until you make up your mind. Make up your mind that you will not just survive your present situation but thrive! Make up your mind that you will find a way to succeed! Make up your mind that you will develop your will to win! It is not only important, but it is critical. Make up your mind—in fact, do it right now!

Mind-set Impacts Wealth

Not only is your mind-set the powerful force that starts you on your journey, but it is also critically important in the process of creating wealth, especially in the midst of financial challenges. Everything depends on your mind-set and your level of determination. You are going to have to be determined to achieve it!

People often confuse determination and persistence because they are so similar, but persistence is an action, while determination is an attitude. When the two combine, dreams become realities! If you want to be a success, you must have a dream, you must decide to follow that dream, and you must make a conscious, determined decision that you will keep going until you achieve that dream, whatever it takes—you must keep going until you achieve it!

I am often asked about the title of my first book, *It Only Takes a Minute to Change Your Life*, and whether you can really change your life in a minute. I always say "Absolutely!" You can definitely change your life in a minute. The minute you make a decision and move in a new direction is the minute you change your life. You might not reach your destination in a minute, but you certainly can change your direction in a minute. The same is true for turning your setbacks into greenbacks—you must first make up your mind!

Get Pressed, Because Pressure Makes Diamonds!

Pressure is a word we all know and a feeling we typically do not like to experience. Most people experience pressure in some form on a daily basis.

The pressure to do well at the office; the pressure of dealing with traffic and getting to and from work; we experience manifold pressures in our daily lives. Over time, we usually adjust to the pressures, and most of the time we learn to handle them. Yet there is something different about financial pressure. Financial pressure can shake our equilibrium. Financial pressure, unchecked, can make you crazy. Yet it is exactly that financial pressure that can be the spark to your developing wealth. It is the pressure that makes diamonds, and can develop a diamond mine for you.

In conversations with my son and his friends, they often use the word *pressed*. In most circles, getting pressed is not seen as something cool. Some believe that it smacks of desperation. Yet, I contend that being pressed and being desperate are two completely different things.

To be pressed is a time of being intense, focused, and determined to win. To be desperate means that you are scattered and are grasping for straws, while drowning in a sea of uncertainty. Pressure makes diamonds while desperation leads to panic and panic leads to disaster. I believe it is necessary and wise to recognize the importance and the power of being pressed. Being pressed is also a time when we move beyond a casual interest in achieving our goals and step up to a level of total commitment. If you are casual, you will become a casualty! I am confident that you must make the decision to move beyond the casual level and get serious, get focused, and get pressed! In tough times, you must step up your game and step up your level of commitment. If you do, you will astound yourself with what you are able to accomplish.

To panic means to take action without thought or a rational plan. To be pressed means to work harder and to work smarter, with a higher level of purpose and conviction. It is okay—in fact it is beneficial—to have times when you are pressed and determined to achieve your goals, but it is a mistake to panic. When people are pressed, they raise their level of activity and intensity, but what is important is how they raise their level. Some people handle pressure by responding to it, while others handle pressure by reacting to it. The difference is that response is positive while reaction is negative.

When you respond to an issue, there is a positive movement, so the impact of the stimulus is positive. The opposite is true with a reaction; there is a negative movement, so the impact of the stimulus is negative. Let's say that a friend of yours has an illness and you take him or her to the hospital. The person is admitted, and the doctor prescribes a medication to treat the illness. Later, when you visit and ask the doctor how your friend is doing, if the doctor says your friend reacted to the medication, you immediately know that it is not good news, yet if the doctor says your friend responded to the medication then you know that it is working and your friend is doing better.

The ability to respond rather than react can be learned. The difference rests primarily in how you perceive and look at life—in other words, it is primarily about your attitude.

Far too often people react to situations and panic, rather than to respond and stay calm. I recommend you respond and stay calm. Practice calmness and stay focused. Be pressed . . . but do not panic!

Pressure creates greater focus and clarity! Great athletes get pressed and get focused if they are behind in the last two minutes of the contest, but they do not panic. Joe Montana, the great quarterback of the San Francisco 49ers, was revered as the king of the two-minute drill. If he was behind, he would calmly gather his troops and tell them to focus and get ready for a two-minute war. Michael Jordan always wanted the ball when his Chicago Bulls were down and someone needed to make the final shot to win. He did not panic; he pressed, and he pushed himself to perform at the next level. Winners make a decision not to panic and fall apart, but instead press and focus all their energies on winning. Are you ready to get through the

11

tough economic times and win? Are you ready to go to war and win? Are you pressed, yet refuse to panic? I hope you say "Yes," because there is no power in a panic!

So, how do you turn that financial pressure into opportunities for greater success? Glad you asked. Just as the earth's pressure can transform a piece of coal into a priceless diamond, so too can the pressures of life transform your situation into a diamond. Pressure makes diamonds . . . but it is critical that you use the pressure for your good, not for your destruction. Pressure makes diamonds, but panic makes destruction.

It is critical that you are focused and determined, pressed to succeed, yet you must not panic because doing so robs you of your ability to think clearly and exercise all your options. And if you cannot select from a clear set of options, your chance of making a *great* choice declines significantly.

Once panic sets in, not only do people tend to make poor choices, they also tend to follow the lead of others who are making poor choices as well.

During the stock market crash of 1929, thousands of people panicked, and it became mass hysteria. It was an epidemic of poor choices and bad decisions. People jumped off buildings and took guns and committed suicide. But, in the end, the market came back, bigger and better than before.

I was amazed at how many people recently panicked when the stock market tanked in 2009. Some people who held stock that had a high of $65 a share panicked when the market fell and hit bottom at $1.05 a share, and they sold their stock at the bottom. Why would anyone sell it then? I have always been told that the secret to success in the stock market is to buy low and sell high. If you didn't sell it when it first started to fall, why in the world would you sell at the bottom? Many people panicked and sold their stock at the bottom . . . and then the stock rose again! So, back to that fundamental first step of turning your economic situation around: make up your mind *not* to panic.

The Realities of Recession

The reality of recession and other economic downturns is that they will come and they will go. Recessions and economic downturns are a part of life, and if we live long enough we will see, from time to time, the economy will struggle. Similarly, we will occasionally have personal recessions; we will see our personal economic status fluctuate. It is a part of the journey of life, and once you have learned to successfully navigate the economic storms, you will come to the realization that a recession is not something to be feared but rather something to be managed.

First, let's look at what a recession is all about. A recession is, by its definition, a general slump in business and an increase in unemployment. It's important to note that both a recession and a depression are economic situations that start with fluctuations in the economic condition of a country or group of countries and then is fueled by fear (corporate fear and then fear of consumers to spend money), which leads to lower sales and eventually to job losses. The cycle keeps going until there is a reduction of the fear and people start to spend again and more money is pushed into the system.

Since the Great Depression, there have been 11 serious recessions and economic downturns, yet in each of those recessions and economic downturns there were people who emerged as millionaires. It was out of the recessions that some were able to create progressions. How did they do it? How can you do it?

Let's start with taking a look at a few people who have become rich as a result of a recession or economic downturn.

Michael J. Cullen

Michael J. Cullen created a new concept called the supermarket during the Great Depression. He moved people away from mom-and-pop grocery stores to a place where they could get everything they wanted under one roof, usually for better prices. He saw an opportunity to help people save money and time, and he prospered during the worst economic situation America has ever seen by thinking and coming up with something that helped people be more successful. His motto was "Pile it high, sell it cheap."

Charles Darrow

You might not know Charles Darrow's name, but you certainly know his invention. He created a little game called *Monopoly* that we still play today. He lost everything in the crash of 1929, but refused to give up and throw in the towel. He worked on an idea for a new board game to help people feel like they were rich. Within a year of the game being released, it sold more than 20,000 units and Darrow became a multimillionaire.

J. Paul Getty

J. Paul Getty used money he received in an inheritance to buy oil stocks after the stock market crash, when the prices were low. He then held them and sold them for a big profit when prices started to rise. He became a billionaire, because he was smart and did what we are all told to do with investments: buy low and sell high!

Howard Hughes

Howard Hughes was a daredevil aviator who took his risk-taking skills to the next level after the stock market crash of 1929. He went on to make films, because he figured people would be willing to pay the price of a movie ticket to escape the gloom and doom of everyday life. He was absolutely right! Then, in the mid-1930s, he thought that people would want to travel once the recession was over, so he started Hughes Aircraft Company and positioned himself as the king of aircraft. Howard Hughes saw a need and took a chance on his vision for the future.

For those of us who were born after the Great Depression, the latest recession has been an interesting lesson in human nature. We have seen people turn from record spending and record credit and debt levels to a change in habits and even a cultural change. We have seen venerable institutional companies like Lehman Brothers go out of business or be bought by their competitors. We have seen companies that were part of our landscape disappear overnight. We have seen people lose their life savings and their long-term investments. We have seen record foreclosures and distress sales. We have seen people lose their jobs, and many of them were unable to find another job for months and months.

We all know people who have been personally affected, and we feel pain for them. It's only natural to hear the daily reports about the bad times and secretly wonder how it will affect us. It can create a malaise that settles over a community, a city, a state, and even a country! But this is not the time to throw our hands in the air and give up; rather, this is a time to look up, think up, and come up with new ideas and strategies to turn this economic setback into a comeback!

We have seen tough times before, and we have come out of each one bigger and better and stronger than we were before the challenge. In each tough situation, people have discovered some specific keys to winning. Even in tough times, there are some who are able to turn the sour lemon of an economy into lemonade. Napoleon Hill, the author of the book *Think and Grow Rich*, said, "Every ADVERSITY, every failure, every heartache, carries with it THE SEEDS OF an equal or greater opportunity!"

Lessons from the Voice of Experience!

I have found that they are some people who have discovered how to get though tough economic times and have come out better than they began. I have had the pleasure of interviewing a good number of individuals who have discovered the

17

secret on my XM Radio show, *The Willie Jolley Wealthy Ways Radio Show*. This show features ideas and insights from some of the world's best and brightest minds on the topic of success and wealth building. Dave Yoho, one of my past interviewees, is a legend in the motivational speaking industry. He is a world-renowned speaker and business consultant who travels around the country sharing his ideas. Even though he is an octogenarian, he has the passion and energy of someone half his age, and is one of the wisest men I have had the pleasure of interviewing.

Born in the 1920s, Dave vividly remembers the stock market crash of 1929 and growing up through that Great Depression. During the interview, he spoke of the important economic lessons he had learned in his 80-plus years, such as the fact that world economies will have good times, followed by tough times; followed by good times, followed by tough times; and then back to good times! Those who succeed over the long term realize that this "came to pass . . . it did not come to stay." Those who understand that setbacks are simply part of the business process are those who thrive; while those who dwell on the changes brought about by setbacks routinely falter. Dave said, "I grew up in a time when we didn't know anything but tough times. We learned that tough times don't last, but tough people do. You must not panic, but keep working on your goals. You can get through these tough times by making a commitment to personal achievement!"

The fact is that setbacks are really simply a part of life, and in life things change . . . and the secret is to not give up! Keep going and keep growing through the challenges. No matter what industry you're in, you're bound to have things change. The key is to remember that these temporary setbacks can empower you to reach even greater levels of business success.

I have talked to other people old enough to remember The Great Depression, and they all say that tough times are a part of life, but we can get through them if we understand the principles. It is not a possibility, but a reality of life. Therefore, it is critical to think through the problem and not to panic.

How to Develop the Power of Calm

Some years ago, there was a deodorant commercial on television that stated that those who are most successful learned to stay cool, calm, and collected. I have to think that message is intended for a lot more than just deodorant. You have a choice when life starts to get crazy: you can get crazy with it, or you can remain calm. The choices you make will have consequences that either help you or hurt you.

I have learned that although many people are aware that it is not good to panic, they continue to panic in the moments of challenge. This is because they do not know how to be calm. Remaining calm in the face of turmoil is a conscious decision, and it must be developed like any other skill. Those who develop the ability to maintain calm in moments of crisis are those who have the greatest amount of success.

Captain Chesley "Sully" Sullenberger has become a national hero because of his ability to remain calm in the midst of potential disaster. He was the pilot of the doomed US Airways plane that lost both engines after being hit by a flock of birds while taking off from LaGuardia Airport in New York. As he flew over Manhattan, he realized he had no engines and no place to land the plane, so he calmly decided to get the plane past Manhattan and try to land it in the Hudson River. He was able to do this successfully, saving the lives of all 155 passengers on board. *The Wall Street Journal* reported that this was the first time in 50 years of commercial jet flight that a pilot was able to successfully execute one of the most technically challenging maneuvers—landing a jetliner in water—without loss of life or major injuries.

Captain Sullenberger said that the first thing he did when he realized he had lost all engines was to decide not to panic and to stay calm and focus his energies. He thought about his options, and when he realized he could not get back to the airport, he decided to land the plane in the water. He said that he "forced himself" to remain calm, because it was only with a calm mind that he would be able to pull off this kind of operation. Many of the people on the plane and their families met with Captain Sullenberger a few weeks after the crash and thanked him profusely for saving their lives and their loved ones. He was humbled by the adulation and the comments, but he said that the key was a decision to remain calm and to think positively and look at the possibilities. Then it became a matter of turning those possibilities into realities. Force yourself to remain calm and think about your possibilities, and then go about turning *your* possibilities into realities.

Think Up, Talk to Yourself, and Talk Power into Your Situation

Most people do not realize the power of positive self-talk. First *think up,* which is to focus on positive, uplifting thoughts. Then you can go to the next level and speak up. Speak goodness into your life and learn to speak power into your situations. For years I have used this technique to encourage myself and to calm myself in the midst of challenging situations. I have found that my own words can give comfort to my mind and my spirit. I make a point of saying to myself, *Stay calm! Stay calm! This is not a big deal! Everything will be all right, just stay calm! You were born for great things, so this is just another character-building experience. Keep going—the best is yet to come!* It sounds so simple, yet it is so very effective. I recommend that you simply try it; you will see that this works. And the more you practice speaking calm into your life, the more you are able to handle challenging situations. Try it for yourself—you will be amazed!

Speak Positivity into Your Life

There will be times when you must use your faith to get to the solution. I believe it is important to learn to speak positivity into your challenges and situations. I've had moments in my life when the circumstances were totally out of my control. At those times, I spoke about my faith and my expectations, and I found that this brought calm into my life and calm into the situation.

For example, once, years ago, I took my mother to get a manicure. While I was waiting, one of the other manicurists convinced me to get my nails cut and buffed. Part of her process was to take hand lotion and massage each hand before cutting the nails. She told me that I needed to remove my wedding ring, but I resisted because I had just celebrated my tenth wedding anniversary, and my wife and I had given each other special diamond rings. She insisted on having me take off my ring, and she went about putting the lotion on my hands and giving them a good once over. As she was finishing, my mother said she needed to get to an appointment. I quickly got up and paid and helped my mother to the car. Of course, I forgot my new wedding anniversary ring!

When I got home, I remembered the ring and tried to call the salon, but it had closed. All I could think about was that I had left the ring on the counter and there were a number of people in line after me, and I began to feel nervous, thinking that one of those people might have picked up my ring. The more I thought about it, the worse it got in my mind. I got to a point where I started to panic, but then I realized that panic was not a healthy response to this situation. I started to speak to myself, and said, *Do not worry! Remember Willie, you are blessed and highly favored! All will be well!* I said that over and over again, and went to bed that night using that statement as a mantra: *Do not worry! Remember Willie, you are blessed and highly favored! All will be well!* The next morning, I went to the salon when it opened and quickly ran to the counter where I had placed my ring—but it was not there. I looked for the lady who had done my nails, but she had not arrived yet. I felt panic trying to get hold of me, but I decided to continue speaking calm into this situation. I continued to repeat my mantra. When the manicurist from the day before walked into the salon, I ran up to her and told her about how I'd left my ring on the counter. She looked at me and shook her head. She then opened her top desk drawer and smiled and said, "Here you are! I put it away for you. I didn't have your number, so I couldn't call you, but I put it safely away for you. I could tell it was important to you, and I wanted to make sure you got it back!" I hugged her, thanked her, and tipped her, and I made a note to remind myself to always remain calm and learn to speak good into life and into challenging situations!

This Too Shall Pass

Throughout the Bible, we see the phrase *it came to pass*, which usually implies that an event or experience came to fulfillment. Yet there is another meaning that I believe is just as powerful in light of these tough times and the numerous challenges associated with them. It means that this situation did not come to stay but rather it came to pass, to move by quickly.

Economic storms, like thunderstorms, come into our lives at various times, but you need to stay mindful of the fact that they come to pass, they do not come to stay . . . and I have been known to exclaim in tough times that "this too shall pass!" I say to you, do not panic and do not jump off any bridges, because this too shall pass. It is not personal and it is not permanent! It came to pass—it did not come to stay. This too shall pass!

Make Good Choices

I saw my friend Donald Cooper, a speaker and trainer from Canada, and he told me a story that his dad used to tell him. His dad told him to be willing to go through the hedge to get to the other side. In the process, there would be scratches and discomfort, but once you made it through, there would be amazing sights and sounds that could not be experienced before going through the hedge. If you make poor choices and don't look to the future with high hopes and high expectations, then you will not position yourself for the amazing things that are possible for the future. Unfortunately, many people panic and make poor decisions and turn small molehills into major mountains that haunt them for years to come. And some make even worse decisions where they end their lives and in doing so they make permanent decisions for temporary problems. Never give up on life because you are in the midst of a storm—the sun will shine again! This storm too shall pass!

Burnt but Blessed . . . Learn to Stay Calm

There are times when life gets hectic and crazy. But that does not mean you must get crazy with it! Those who win in life are those who are able to stay calm in the midst of life's craziness. The more you practice staying calm, the more you will stay calm in a moment of crisis.

I had a moment of crisis when my car caught on fire. I had traveled to Wisconsin and Minnesota to speak. My wife, Dee, chose not to travel with me, because she was attending a women's retreat in Virginia. She also had to teach our communication skills class that Sunday at our church. She had driven our late-model Mercedes to Williamsburg, Virginia, and back to Washington, D.C. She picked me up from the airport on Monday. We went to the resort at National Harbor, Maryland, for an afternoon program. After the program, we decided to stop by our church for the last part of Bible study.

After Bible study, while I was speaking to the pastor, someone rushed in and said, "Willie, your car is on fire!" We rushed to the parking lot, and sure enough, our car was ablaze.

According to the police, our car had started smoking. Then sparks and flames began to come from under the hood, as well as the dashboard. The police called the fire department. Since the electrical system was burned and disabled, they could not open the doors or the hood of the car. They had to use an axe to break open the windows and to get the hood open to put out the fire.

As we stood there, watching our car being consumed by flames, someone asked how we were doing. I said, "I am blessed and grateful! This is nothing but a minor setback; and a setback is nothing but a setup for a comeback!"

"You really believe that stuff you talk about, don't you?" he asked. My reply was, "You are absolutely right! This is not a big deal. See, this car could have caught fire while Dee was driving to her conference, to our class, to pick me up from the airport, to take me to my program, or while we were driving to church tonight! I am blessed and so very grateful. And, I know the world will not end. It is just a car. I can replace a car. I can't replace my wife!"

People were amazed that I was so calm. But what they did not know is that I *learned* to stay calm and not let external issues disrupt my internal joy and peace. Happiness is typically a result of the "happenings" in your life. But joy is the result of your internal positioning, and I decided long ago that I would not let "stuff" steal or disrupt my joy!

You, too, can develop calmness within, even in the midst of crazy times. How? One technique is to make a commitment to say calming things to yourself. Practice being calm by saying aloud, "Stay calm and do not panic!" Then ask yourself: *Will the world stop turning because of this problem?* If the answer is no, keep moving!

By the way, I want to tell you the rest of the story. I truly believe a setback is nothing but a setup for a comeback, and you must keep calm and keep the faith. As I told you, our car was a late-model Mercedes, and when I told the folks at Mercedes what had happened, they went to work and delivered a special edition Mercedes for us that was much nicer and had more bells and whistles than our original vehicle. That is why you must not panic nor lose heart, because a setback is truly a setup for a comeback!

Settle Down and Think Up

When life throws us curveballs, they can come in a wave, and they can certainly create waves in their wake. Once the rush of activity begins, we can easily get caught up in the activity, and if we are not mindful, we can get caught up in a mob mentality, the hysteria of the moment. These are times when people get caught up in activities without really thinking them through, yet they do them anyway, because everyone else is doing them. It typically happens in a rushing wave, in which people act before they think. When a herd stampedes, it's because each single cow is carried along with the crowd. We have seen soccer mobs exhibit crazy behavior and fight each other over stupid stuff, and later have no idea why they did what they did. They cannot explain it, they only can describe that it was "so quick that I didn't know what was happening! I just got caught up!" That is exactly why it is important to stay calm, even when others around you are losing their minds. I make a point of practicing calm even when the people around me are getting overly excited about the issues that are swirling around and about them. Stay calm!

Develop a Sound Mind

For God has not given us a spirit of fear, but of power and love and of a sound mind!
—*2 Tim 1:6*

Talk yourself into a calm, controlled state of thinking and acting. Develop a calm, composed, sound mind. And whatever you do, remember that God has blessed you with life, power, the ability to love, and the option of maintaining a sound, calm mind. Remember, remaining calm is a choice . . . so I recommend you use it and not lose it.

Talk to yourself, and learn to talk yourself into a calm and controlled way of thinking and acting. It is critical that you do not lose your composure, because once you've lost your composure, you have lost the battle!

Broke, Busted, and Disgusted

When we are broke, everything becomes magnified. Our molehill-sized problems become mountains and our pains become more pronounced. We can go from broke to busted to plain old disgusted. And we know that tough times can affect people in many different ways. When people lose their jobs, their homes, or their life savings, they also lose their sense of personal security. I have found that when I begin to feel overwhelmed by the state of current affairs, or when I am hit with personal problems that can have an impact on my sanity, I need to step back and recover so that I can get back into the fight.

First, let me say that success is a fight. It is not going to be easy; if it were easy, everyone would do it. Someone said that in life, you either have a problem, you have just left a problem, or you are on your way to a problem. Life is challenging, yet it is worth the fight!

What should you do if you are depressed? First you need to find if your depression is chemical or emotional. A chemical depression needs to be addressed by a medical professional, because it is a medical issue and needs medical attention. Yet some depression is the result of emotional distress due to the effect of overwhelming negative information on our psyche and our perspective of the world. Studies have shown that a constant barrage of negative input can alter our emotional state and our outlook on life. We have all experienced tough days when "Murphy" comes to visit. (You know Murphy's Law: anything that can go wrong will go wrong, at the worst possible time.) When you have those moments, I recommend you make a decision to respond to the feelings and move on them, before they move on you.

When life throws you serious setbacks and depression tries to overtake you, it is critical that you reframe your thinking. Here are a few simple steps that I recommend.

Change Your Environment

Leave the place where you are, and change the texture of the environment. Maybe you can take a walk, take a drive, or go to a different area of your house or building. The key is to change the input of the moment and get some new input and new perspective. The change can have a tremendous effect on your emotions.

A few years ago, when my Aunt Eunice died, I started to feel a sense of depression come over me. Aunt Eunice was like a second mother to me, and when my mom died after a long illness, Aunt Eunice became a surrogate mother. I talked to her every week. When she died, it hit me pretty hard, and I realized I needed to reframe my thinking, so I told my staff I would be back and I went for a nice long ride in my car through Rock Creek Park, which is near my office. As I noticed the beautiful scenery, I had a conversation with myself, and asked myself the questions that I often share with families who lose loved ones: "Are you going to curse because a rose bush has thorns? Or are you going to celebrate because a thorn bush has roses? Are you going to curse because your loved one is gone, or are you going to celebrate because your loved one came this way?" I realized that I needed to celebrate the years I had with Aunt Eunice. As I thought about the fact that I had been blessed to have Aunt Eunice in my life, I started to feel better. Then I thought about one of my favorite quotes, from noted author and poet Maya Angelou. Ms. Angelou said, "If you don't like something, change it. If you can't change it, change your attitude." I could not change the circumstances, so I decided to change my attitude, and it changed my thinking and my mood.

Reframe Your Thinking with an Attitude of Gratitude

Another powerful technique to beat the blues and overcome the spirit of depression is to think about the things in your life for which you are grateful. Take a moment and focus on the things that you have, rather than the things that you don't have. As my friend W. Mitchell said after he was paralyzed in an airplane accident, "Before I was paralyzed, there were 10,000 things I could do. Now there are 9,000. I can either dwell on the 1,000 I've lost or focus on the 9,000 I have left."

Another technique to help you cultivate an attitude of gratitude is to add the words "at least" to the end of the sentence when you are talking about the challenges that are trying to bring you down. For example: "My pay got cut, but at least I still have a job" or "I lost my job, but at least I still have my health!" Or, "I am sick, but at least I am still here!" When you add the phrase "at least" to the end of the sentence, you are changing your thinking. It provides you with another perspective, a positive perspective, and from there you can start to reframe your thinking and overcome the grip of depression. When you have an attitude of gratitude, you see life from a different perspective. Every day is a holiday. Every meal is a feast, and every drink of water is a toast to the magnificent journey of life and love. Live your life with an attitude of gratitude!

Think about Helping Others

This sounds so simplistic, but it is so incredibly impactful. Social scientists have found that changing your focus from yourself to helping others can be beneficial in overcoming depression. By looking at others and finding ways that you can help them, you can see that you are a valuable part of the culture and can become a helpful force of nature. Focusing your attention and energy on others can minimize your issues and help you realize how blessed you are. It's like the old saying, "I was feeling sorry for myself because I had no shoes until I met a person who had no feet." If you deflect your attention from your own problems and open your eyes to the situations and circumstances of those around you, you will find an opportunity to help others and, while doing so, help yourself!

I recommend you try to uplift others and encourage others, as it can have a tremendous impact on you. I feel that if you are willing to help others and spray a little perfume on them, you cannot help but get a little bit on you as well.

Change Your Input

Another way to beat back depression and change your mood is to change your input! Your input determines your output. Rather than dwelling on the negative input that started you on the path to depression, I recommend you shift your attention away from the things that have sent you in the direction of depression and focus your attention elsewhere.

For me, music is a tremendous tool to help lift my spirits. In fact, I make it a habit to listen to uplifting music every day, no matter what is going on in my life; it always makes me feel better. At times, it pulls me out of a low point and helps me regain my equilibrium and return to a point of normalcy.

I'll never forget a time, some years ago, when I was in Annapolis, Maryland, to speak for a big hotel event. The event was during the evening, and I had come in the night before to spend some time at the hotel and learn more about the employees' culture. After a tour in the morning, I had the afternoon off, and I went back to my room and turned on the television while I was getting ready to get some work done. The movie *Selena* had just started and it captured my attention. I had heard about this beautiful young lady who became a superstar in the Hispanic community. It was an intriguing story, and because of the great music, I was drawn to it. I sat and watched the whole film, and then, at the end, this beautiful young lady was killed by a deranged fan. I watched as her family mourned and the community grieved, and I was overtaken by an overwhelming sense of sadness. I was depressed! And then I realized that I had about an hour before I was to speak before all of these people in the hotel ballroom. I knew I had to get over this depression and had to do it quickly, so I pulled out my iPod and put on "You've Got to Keep Kicking," a song written by my friend Tony Taylor that had been featured on one of my earlier albums. I listened to the song, and immediately, the sadness dissipated and I started to feel better. As I listened to more of the songs in my "power play list," I got stronger and stronger, and in a short time I was back, and ready to go out and fire up that audience!

In the Bible, it is noted that King Saul suffered from depression, and whenever that "distressing spirit" came upon him, he would call on David to come and play his harp to lift him out of his distress. Inspirational and uplifting music can brighten your day and give you hope, and when you have hope for the future it can give you power in the present! The much–loved quotation is absolutely true: "Music hath charms to soothe a savage beast, to soften rocks, or bend a knotted oak!"

Fill Yourself with the Pure, the Powerful, and the Positive

Another way to reframe your thinking and beat depression is to fill yourself with the pure, the powerful, and the positive. Create a list of affirmations and quotations that align with your value system to lift your spirits. I often rely on Scriptural references, such as, "If God be for us, who can be against us?" (Rom 8:31 NKJV) or "But they that wait upon the Lord shall renew their strength; they shall mount up with wings as eagles; they shall run, and not be weary; and they shall walk, and not faint" (Isaiah 40:31 NKJV).

I recommend having a list of motivational and inspirational quotes or phrases that you can apply to challenging situations. Of course, my favorites are:

- A setback is nothing but a setup for a comeback!

- The best is yet to come.
- No matter what, I know that I am blessed and highly favored!
- When I am down to nothing, I know that God is up to something.
- No matter what the situation, God and I make a majority!

I have learned that we must speak power into our lives, because our words have an impact on our thinking and our feeling! So I recommend you memorize scriptural and inspirational quotes to help you fight the drama of depression.

Rest and Rejuvenate

Another remedy for depression is a simple, yet effective solution, and that is to rest and renew yourself. Sometimes, you need to get away and get some rest and rejuvenation so you can get back into the fight. I remember after one particularly trying day, I talked with my friend Greg Owen, an entrepreneur and success expert who lives in Sydney, Australia. Greg said, "Willie, this has been a tough fight, so I am going to go take an aspirin and lie down, and when I wake up I will be ready to fight again!"

Sometimes you just need to rest and renew yourself. We are all human, and we all get tired and need to rest to rejuvenate ourselves. Learn to get proper rest, exercise, and a proper diet, and it can have a profound impact on your battle with depression.

Some people have said that super success is the result of either inspiration or desperation, and I believe there is some truth in that statement. Sometimes we get our best ideas in extreme situations, when we are pressed to win and do not panic. There is a thin line between being pressed and being panicked, but it is a line that winners learn they cannot cross. Just as there is a thin line between confidence and arrogance, a person who is successful learns where that line is and develops the discipline not to cross it.

Bob Johnson, the billionaire businessman who founded Black Entertainment Television, said, "The same hammer that shatters the glass, forges the steel!" We will all have challenges and difficulties in our lives, but we must develop ourselves so that we are able to not just go through those challenges, but grow through those challenges. Our responses to life's challenges determine how the pressures of life affect us. These pressures can build us up or break us down. I recommend that you use the pressures of life to build you and make you into the diamond you were born to be! Don't just *go* through it, *grow* through it! Do not panic!

Make Up Your Mind . . . Get Pressed, but Do Not Panic

My good friend, speaker and author Dr. Terry Paulson, has a great book called *The Optimism Advantage: 50 Simple Truths to Transform Your Attitude and Actions into Results* (John Wiley & Sons, Inc., 2010). In the book, he does a tremendous job of helping use optimism to create massive success and wealth. He writes:

> Claiming the optimism advantage is not motivational hype. Optimism is an attitude that is earned through a track record of overcoming obstacles. The more setbacks and adversity you have handled, the more you come to believe that you can overcome the next one life gives you. Tough times can be the launching pad for great success. Optimists are realists who are problem solvers, not problem evaders. They want to know what obstacles they are facing so that they can get busy finding a solution. Optimists understand that wealth is really the intersection of income and impact. The more you see yourself solving problems, the more you go about the work and the more money becomes available to you. Make a point of making the commitment to turn your worry into constructive action every day. Take it one day at a time, just take it and make it happen. Every successful

entrepreneur will tell you that the journey to wealth is filled with closed doors, setbacks, failures, and the satisfying joy of achieving success along the way. Don't let anyone call you a victim; you are a resilient survivor who is choosing to live your dream. Wealth is not the only goal; in reality it is the byproduct of transforming our gifts into a mission that makes a difference people are willing to pay for. When you find your gifts, identify your mission, and claim a positive attitude, wealth and meaning are on the way!

Don't Willingly Participate or Commiserate

I like to say, "Too many people follow the crowd, even if the crowd is going in the wrong direction." That being said, I encourage you to decide that you will not willingly participate or commiserate, and the definitive word in this statement is "willingly."

For many years when I spoke about economic downturns, I would quickly say, "I am not participating in this recession!" I was fine with that until I realized that everyone feels the impact of tough economic times. Also, I realized that telling someone who just lost his or her home or retirement savings to "not participate" was somewhat disingenuous. It was not meant to be disingenuous, but nevertheless, it was hard to tell someone who was living a terrible financial nightmare to just ignore what was going on in his or her life. In my heart, I wanted to tell people, "Do not buy into the doom and gloom and the bad news and negative thinking!" But you cannot avoid the impact of some events in life, no matter how hard you try.

I had to think about my message and come up with a statement that was clearer, one that conveyed strength and a caring message for those who had been involuntarily sucked into an economic mess. As I thought about it, I realized that we cannot choose to be pulled into economic downturns, but we can choose not to participate willingly! In other words, we do not have to get in line and go along with the program. We need not add fuel to a raging fire. We need not contribute to the problem, but rather we should be part of the solution.

When we willingly participate, we become volunteer victims! A volunteer victim is someone who voluntarily positions themselves for victimhood. I was watching *The Apprentice* television show with Donald Trump, and he had a similar take on getting in line with those who are willing to lose. A contestant was part of the team that lost, but she did not contribute to the team losing. Yet to be supportive of the team leader, she volunteered to go back in the boardroom with the team leader, even though she was not one of the culprits that caused the loss. When Trump asked why she was back in the boardroom, he was told she volunteered. He immediately fired her! He said, "Never voluntarily get in the line for execution! Don't even get close to the area if you do not have to!" It was a tough lesson, but it was true. Far too many people get in line for execution with tough economies when they need not do so. Do not get in line with all the people who have decided to buy into the gloom and doom of the times. Do not be like sheep who are lining up to go to slaughter!

I believe that being a willing participant is like walking around with a "Kick Me" sign taped to your back. Life will kick you, and keep kicking you if you allow it to do so. I often say that life looks for people it can knock down and keep down; those who are defiant are those who make life leave them alone. If you are willing to fight back and be defiant, life will typically leave you alone and go look for a wimp to keep down.

I travel a lot, and on one trip I got to the airport and needed to quickly check my luggage and get to my flight. It was a cold winter day, so I immediately went to the inside check-in area to check my luggage, but the line was super long. I knew that because of this I would not be able to catch my flight; I needed to look for other options. I buttoned up my coat and went outside, because there is usually a curbside check-in option. It was cold, but there was a much shorter line. I quickly checked my luggage and was off to catch my flight.

As I walked past the line inside, there was a young lady who was anxiously looking at her watch with a pained look on her face. I stopped and asked her if everything was okay. She said she had been in the line for a long time and needed to check her luggage. I asked her why she was in the line when there were other options, and she

Don't Willingly Participate or Commiserate

responded, "Because everyone else was in the line!" I called the skycap who had just helped me and asked him if he would help her. He looked at her ticket and said, "Too late! That flight has already closed!" Turns out she missed her flight because she got in line with all the other folks, thinking there were no other options.

In life, don't get in line with the other people . . . check out the options. Jesus taught, "And if the blind lead the blind, both shall fall into a ditch" (Matthew 15:14 NKJV). I encourage people to look at all the options and make the decision that works best for them. Take the "Kick Me" sign off your back, and make up your mind that you will not willingly participate (rather than participate willingly) in economic downturns, recessions, depressions, or anything else. You might feel it, but you need not be a willing party to it. Too many people follow the crowd, even if the crowd is going in the wrong direction.

We do not have to go along with the status quo without at least giving a fight. Les Brown has a statement that I love: "Life is a fight for territory. When you stop fighting for what you want, what you don't want automatically takes over!" It is in these moments of challenge that we will either move forward toward our goals and dreams or we will fall back towards our fears. The choice literally is up to you! It is in these moments that we must

Turn Setbacks into Greenbacks

look at encouraging ourselves to get off the canvas of life and get back in the fight. It is wonderful if you have a team of people cheering you on, but sometimes you have no one to help you get up but yourself. That is why it is critical to learn to have positive conversations with yourself. We can make up our minds that we will go kicking and screaming, and will not stop fighting. Do not go down without a fight! In other words, I am telling you that it is important that you be unreasonable and defiant! That's right, be unreasonable and be defiant! You must be willing to fight for your goals. Think about people who say they want to reach their goals, yet they act like they will do it only if it's easy. That is how most people act about their goals; they will work toward their goal only if it is not an inconvenience. No! That is not the way to achieve your goal. You must want it and must be willing to fight to make it a reality.

I have said for years that you must be unreasonable to get what you want in life. To be unreasonable does not mean being rude or nasty, but rather that you will not take "no" for an answer. You will not give up on your dreams and goals just because others cannot see your vision. If it is not other people, it will be the circumstances of life that will suggest that you should just accept the status quo, the way things are. I say you must be willing to be unreasonable. Life will say, "Just be reasonable

Don't Willingly Participate or Commiserate

and accept this situation," but I reply with, "*No*, that is not acceptable, and I cannot accept that option." Again, you need not be rude or nasty to take a stand. You simply need to make up your mind that you will not willingly participate. To beat a recession or economic downturn, you must be willing to fight, fight for your dreams and goals, and keep fighting.

The Bible says that we are to have life and have it more abundantly, not less abundantly. The recession, the depression, and all the other economic calamities are not the way God wants us to live. That is why I wake up every morning and give God thanks for another day and another opportunity to live my dreams, not my fears. That is why I give God glory every day for life and the opportunity to make a difference and make a profit. That is why I wake up every day and say, "Good morning, Lord!" rather than "Oh Lord, it's morning!" That is why I say, every day, "This is going to be a great day, because I have life and I can choose to make it a great day!" I cannot choose what happens to me, and I cannot choose what happens around me, but I have complete choice about what happens in me . . . and I choose to be happy, grateful, and excited about this upcoming day!

Do not get in line with all the people who have decided to buy into the gloom and doom of the times.

When you make up your mind that you will not willingly participate, you change the game and resist being sucked in by all the bad news and gloom and doom that are a part of the media spin. That media spin will not only influence you but can have an impact on you for years to come.

I saw an old friend with whom I'd grown up, and I asked about his brother, who was my elementary school playmate. My old friend asked if I would call his brother, because his brother had been going through some tough times and needed some encouragement to get back up on his feet. I said I would be happy to do so, and made the call. After a few initial greetings with my old classmate, I said, "So I saw your brother, and he asked me to call. How are things going?" My old classmate responded, "Things are not going too well. I have been out of work for a long time, and I am way behind on my bills." I then asked, "Where have you been looking for work?" He responded, "Well, I haven't been looking." I said, "Why not?" His response amazed me. He said, "I haven't been looking because the people on television say there are no jobs!" Unfortunately, many people buy into this thinking, because they trust the news media as the truth tellers of the society, when really they are sharing a perspective, their perspective of the truth.

Yes, it is true that in tough times it is harder to get a job, yet it is not impossible to get a job.

Don't Willingly Participate or Commiserate

How do I know? Well, while people here in America are talking about not being able to get a job, people who come here from other countries are often not only getting one job but are getting multiple jobs! These jobs might not be the top of the line, but they are a way to keep your bills paid until you can get a top-of-the-line job. When people say, "There are no jobs," I always wonder . . . if there are no jobs, why is there still a need for newspaper employment advertisements? There are still pages and pages of jobs being advertised every day. My old classmate had bought into the gloom and the doom! He had become a willing participant in the bad times. Network marketing expert Hope Elliott said to me when I came to speak for her group, "POOR is Passing Over Opportunities Regularly!" Open your mind to possibilities and do not buy into the gloom and doom. Remember, sometimes opportunities will knock on the door and we will say, "Stop making all that noise, go away!" Open your eyes and your mind to the great opportunities that are all around you!

The secret to succeeding is a willingness to think beyond the gloom and doom and look for opportunities. You must not become a willing participant in the economic downturn. You must fight back and keep fighting back!

Don't Commiserate

The word *commiserate* is a word we usually think of when we have people who sit around and bemoan their favorite sports team losing a big game, but when striving for success in the face of setbacks, the word also has impact. I want to warn you against commiserating in the game of life. The practice of going around talking about how bad things are to people in your network will get you nowhere. Often, when bad things happen in life, we find people who make a habit of going around talking about the bad things—and that is all they do. It adds fuel to a raging fire and creates a doom and gloom scenario and a victim mentality.

People who commiserate are the ones who call and tell you all the bad news of the day: "Did you hear the bad news about Company X going out of business?" or, "Did you hear about Company Y laying off more people?" Woe is me, woe is me.

People who commiserate are the people who would rather complain about problems than to do anything to fix them. We have a choice. We can talk about all the bad news and keep repeating it, or we can go about making a difference and being a light in a dark world. We can be people who complain and do nothing else or people who stop complaining about what we allow. It is like the story of the old farmer who was sitting on his porch with his old hound dog. The dog was just sitting there howling. A stranger came by and asked the old farmer why the dog was howling and making so much noise, and the old farmer replied, "Because he is sitting on a nail."

The stranger asked, "Why doesn't he get up?"

The old farmer responded, "Because it doesn't hurt badly enough!"

Many people will get in the line and complain about the situation but will not do much to change the circumstances. You must make the decision to stay away from the negative talkers who do nothing but talk. Talking about problems without offering solutions creates a lose/lose scenario. It is important that you do not allow yourself to get into the trap of complaining about a situation in your life without offering a solution to the problem.

Commiserating can have an impact on your psyche and your emotional stability. A constant barrage of negative information can lead to a negative view of the world.

Commiserating can create a psychological construct, a self-fulfilling prophecy—a situation that is not yet true but has the potential to become true, because you have created an expectation that it will become reality. The more you talk about bad news, the deeper its impact will be on your psyche and your physiology, and the more your mind moves to make it a reality. Scripture says, "For as he thinks in his heart, so is he." (Proverbs 23:7 NKJV).

A study was done at the University of Texas regarding the impact of bad news on the psyche and physiology of athletes. A football player was selected to be one of the case studies. After practice, he was asked by a researcher, "How are you doing?" He responded, "Outstanding! Fired up! It was a great practice and I am ready to take on the world!" The person in the study responded by saying, "Are you sure? You look a little sick!" The football player replied, "No, I feel great!"

A short while later, the football player was approached by a different person associated with the study and asked the same question. The football player responded, "I feel fine." The person in the study said, "All right, but you look a little sick." Over the next few hours, different people stopped the football player and asked the same set of questions and gave the same "you look sick" response. By the end of the day, the football player was feeling sick and depressed, because he had been inundated with so much gloom and doom and bad news about his health. In reality, he was not sick, but the high level of negative news made him think he was. It is critical that you stay away from the gloom-and-doomers and the negative provocateurs!

Don't Willingly Participate or Commiserate

I met a gentleman one day who had seen me on television. He came up to me and started rattling off about how bad things were for his business and business in general. He said, "Did you hear about how bad things are here and how bad things are there? Did you hear that so-and-so lost their business? Did you hear?" Before he could get a full head of steam, I stopped him and said, "If you are looking for someone to commiserate with, you've got the wrong guy. I am aware that there are some tough situations all around, but I decided I am not going to dwell on the problems. Instead, I am thinking and looking at all the great opportunities. Now is the time when the winners are made! I am working harder than ever, and I am planning to have my best year yet. I realize there are some challenges out in the business world; but wherever there are challenges, there are opportunities. I am planning to work hard and find those opportunities, and I cannot find any opportunities if I continue to look at the situation as hopeless. I will be like Hannibal, the great African military man, who said, 'If you cannot find a way, make a way!' Hannibal could find no way to defeat the Romans with a frontal attack, so he did the unthinkable: He used African elephants to transport his troops over the Alps and attacked the Romans from the rear, and he defeated them because when there was no opportunity he decided to create an opportunity. Now is the time to create some great new opportunities."

I realized that part of the reason this man's business was suffering was because he was dwelling on the negatives about business, rather than the positives. If you focus on the negative points in your life, those are what will grow, but the same is true for the positive. Be aware of the negative issues, but focus on the positive, the possibilities. Whatever you focus on and think about is what you will become and what you will grow.

Make a point that you will not sign up, line up, or whine up about the recession but you will stand up and fight for your dreams and goals, and never, ever give up on you and the incredible possibilities that are within you!

Don't Let Your Pride Poison Your Prosperity

If you are going to turn your setbacks into greenbacks, it is necessary to get past your pride and make the decision that you will not let your pride poison your prosperity. Do not let pride get in the way of your becoming wealthy. Pride is an interesting word, because we all are expected to have self-respect and pride in ourselves, but too much pride can keep us from achieving our goals and dreams. Pride can create conceit and an unwillingness to try new ideas. I want to concentrate on this point. Pride left unchecked can alter your view of the world and your perspective on taking advantage of the opportunities that will help you grow your success.

To turn a setback into a financial comeback will take some new thinking and some new actions, because it is true that if you keep doing what you have been doing, you will keep getting what you have been getting. You have to do some different things, and do some things differently. Often, what stops people from success is not their ability but their pride. They are overly concerned about what "people" will say. To that, I say that to turn your setbacks into greenbacks, you cannot worry about what people will say but rather what your heart will say! Did you give your best? Did you give your

61

all? Did you have integrity and character? Did you hold up your end of the bargain with God? Did you remember that God's gift to you is life, and your gift to God is what you do with your life? As Martin Luther King Jr. said, "If a man is called to be a street sweeper, he should sweep streets as Michelangelo painted, and Shakespeare wrote poetry! He should sweep streets so well that all the hosts of heaven will proclaim, 'there lived a great street sweeper who did his job well!'" You cannot let pride stand in the way of your wealth!

Far too often, I see people who are struggling financially but not doing anything to turn their finances around because they are trying to put up a façade of success. As my friend Larry Winget, the host of the television show *Big Spender*, says, "There are a lot of people who could turn their lives around, but they have too much pride, and therefore they are too stupid to become wealthy. They are putting on an act that they are doing well, when they can hardly pay their basic bills. They are $30,000 millionaires! Big hat, no cattle!"

You cannot let your pride get in the way of your wealth building. Some people feel that some work is beneath them. They feel that it would bring a stigma to them if people know they were doing supposedly "demeaning" work, yet they struggle to pay their bills. I believe any work that is moral and legal is honorable.

Working through a Downturn

My friend Duke Greene is a great example of how to build wealth and not get stuck on minor issues, and instead stay focused on the major ones. Duke Greene was a guest on my XM Radio show and shared a story that had the phones ringing off the hook. He told how he started the company IBS (International Business Services) in the 1970s, built it into a national powerhouse, and then sold it in the 1990s. The company was worth $96 million, and he had offices all across the country with thousands of employees. However, during an economic downturn in the 1970s, he made up his mind that he did not want to lose any of the great people he had hired, so he decided not to lay off any of his people. As the CEO, he was the highest paid person on the payroll, so he took his salary and contributed it to help pay the employees. After a few months of living on his savings, he realized he needed to do something to pay his personal bills. He knew that the economic downturn was a temporary situation and that the economy would come back, so he just needed to get through the tough months. So he worked all day as the CEO of IBS, and at night he drove a truck, like he had done in college, to make ends meet. He said that leaders do not let the circumstances stop

Don't Let Your Pride Poison Your Prosperity

them from doing what is necessary to grow their businesses. As long as it is moral and legal, it is good business and honorable work.

Someone called in to ask a question after Duke shared his story. They said, "What if you have been a professional and now you have to do something that is beneath you?" Duke responded, "You have to get over it! You have to realize that this is temporary! It is not forever, it is just something you have to do to pay your bills and get through the tough times!"

I know that economic downturns and slow times in business can be overwhelming, but if you do not panic, but instead look for opportunities, you will see that they are all around you. If you can get past what people will think about you on the front end, you will find that they will have great respect for you on the back end!

From the Ground Up

Years ago, I was invited to speak at the Wendy's Restaurant Leadership Conference in Fort Lauderdale, Florida. The conference was created by the founder of Wendy's, Dave Thomas. Dave was still alive at the time, and when his office called and asked if I would be the keynote speaker for their conference, I was thrilled and gladly accepted. As a part of the weekend, we were told that Dave Thomas would like to have us over for dinner the night before the conference. So my wife and I flew to Fort Lauderdale the day before the conference and had dinner with Dave Thomas at his waterside mansion.

During dinner I asked Dave how he started Wendy's. His answer is an incredible testament to the power of not letting pride poison your prosperity. Dave told me that he was adopted, and during his teen years he got a job at a local restaurant. He said he loved the restaurant business and as a result he dropped out of school so he could work more hours. His friends laughed at him and told him it was embarrassing to work at the restaurant, scrubbing floors and flipping burgers. In fact they laughed at him and called him "Hamburger Boy!" But Dave didn't care. He made up his mind that he was not going to let what others thought of him be the thing that determined his destiny.

During his time at the restaurant, Dave met an older gentleman named Harland Sanders who had started a restaurant chain called Kentucky Fried Chicken. Dave ended up taking over some of the struggling Kentucky Fried Chicken restaurants in the Ohio area and turned them around. He sold those restaurants and then decided to start a hamburger restaurant with custom-made hamburgers. He named the restaurant after his daughter,

Wendy—and the rest is history! Dave went on to become one of the most successful businessmen in American history and the most successful founder-turned-television spokesman ever.

Dave Thomas did not let his pride poison his prosperity. He was a high school dropout who never stopped thinking about his goals and dreams and was willing to work hard to make his dreams become realities. He was proud of going back to school and passing his General Educational Development (GED) tests, but he was most noted for his hard work and his MBA, which is what he called his "Mop and Bucket Attitude." No job was beneath him, and all work was honorable, as long as it didn't offend the laws of God or the laws of the land.

And by the way, many of those people who laughed at him and called him "Hamburger Boy" ended up calling him "Boss!" He was able to make those who laughed at him on the front end eat their words and work for him on the back end. Do not be concerned about what others think of you; focus on your dreams and goals!

Take Out the Trash

Another example of someone who did not let his pride poison his prosperity is Wayne Huizenga.

Wayne Huizenga made his wealth as a trash man. He was born during the Great Depression and grew up poor. As a young man, he started working for a family who had a trash company. After a couple of years, he had saved enough money to buy his own trash truck, and he started his own company. Many laughed at him because he was a trash man, but he never let his pride get in the way of his prosperity. He would pick up trash from 2:00 A.M. until midday, and for the rest of the day he would go door to door to drum up business. He bought more trash trucks, hired more people, and eventually bought his biggest competitor. Eventually, Huizinga's company, Waste Management, Inc. went public. He continued to grow the business; eventually he became wealthy and even bought the Miami Dolphins football team and the Florida Marlins baseball team. He went from hauling trash to hauling millions of dollars to the bank, because he refused to let others determine his possibilities. He refused to let his pride poison his prosperity.

Let me say this emphatically: You must not let what other people think about you stop you from taking action. Often we get stymied and end up doing nothing because of our pride. We can get overwhelmed by fear or low expectations, but these can create a lack of activity and therefore a lack of success. It is critical that you make up your mind, get going, and take some action.

Don't Let Your Pride Poison Your Prosperity

So what should we do? Something, anything . . . just move forward! You can't sit there waiting for success to come to you. If you fail, then try again, start over and keep trying, just do something positive toward your goal. Don't wait or it just may be too late! Take action! And remember . . . massive success is always the best revenge!

STEP 4

Don't Stop Thinking and Dreaming about the Power and Possibilities of Tomorrow

> The future belongs to those who believe in the beauty of their dreams!
>
> —*Eleanor Roosevelt*

The next step in turning your setbacks into greenbacks is "Don't stop thinking about the possibilities of tomorrow." This concept is taken from the Fleetwood Mac song, which has become one of the top songs on my iPod favorites play list. I had heard the song years ago, but never really listened to the lyrics, yet when I took time to really listen, I realized it was my kind of song . . . something that would uplift and inspire people to live better!

If you listen, you will find that the song implores us to keep going and keep thinking about the future, because those who keep working on their goals typically create better futures. When things are tough and we are feeling low, we need to look up and think up, so that we can see things differently and recognize new possibilities. Don't stop, don't give up on your dreams and goals. . . . Keep thinking about tomorrow and the better days to come. The chorus of the song implores us to

Don't Stop Thinking and Dreaming

have a positive outlook, positive in-look, and positive up-look!

This concept of Don't Stop Thinking About Tomorrow has multiple meanings that can best be demonstrated by the "Inflection Emphasis Communications Technique." In this technique, the way you emphasize the different words in the statement—*Don't. Stop. Thinking. About. Tomorrow*—can alter the meaning of the statement.

A few years ago, my wife and I started teaching a class on communications skills at our church, and we used a resource called Speaking with Bold Assurance, developed by Bert Decker. Bert is a friend and one of the top media coaches in the country. In this program, he taught about the power of inflection and emphasis, and how in communications the word you choose to emphasize can have a tremendous impact on the meaning of the statement. Bert uses the phrase "I. Didn't. Say. You. Stole. That. Car." I want you to repeat this statement out loud seven times, and each time, I want you to put the emphasis on a different word. First emphasize the word *I* in the statement; the next time, emphasize the word *didn't*. On the third time, emphasize the word *say*, and so on. You will see that the meaning of the statement drastically changes depending on where you place the emphasis.

If we follow the same process for the statement "Don't stop thinking about tomorrow," we will see that the messages that are generated are all different. Yet they all apply in helping you turn your economic setbacks into greenbacks!

First is the word *don't*. *Don't* stop thinking about tomorrow! To turn your setbacks into greenbacks, it is critical for you to be dogmatic in your thinking about coming back. You must not even consider that you will not be able to get through this tough stretch. Don't even think about it! Don't let the negative thoughts get in your mind. Oh, they might try to invade your thoughts—but you, ultimately, control your thinking. Norman Vincent Peale, author of the book, *The Power of Positive Thinking*, said, "You may not be able to keep birds from flying above your head, but you don't have to let them build a nest." Negative thoughts will fly all around your mind, but don't even consider that you will not be able to survive this economic situation. You must stay positive, and if you have to talk to yourself and encourage yourself, so be it! Get a *don't* mindset, and by the pure nature of the word, you will become more willing to keep fighting.

By placing the emphasis on the word *stop*, the focus shifts to the fact that you must keep hitting the rock, keep pushing, and keep trying to achieve your goals. As you keep hitting the rock, you know that if you hit it long enough and hard enough it will eventually break! Once the rock, the hard obstacle in front of you, breaks, you will not know

73

Don't Stop Thinking and Dreaming

for sure whether it broke because the hundredth hit was so powerful that it shattered the rock, or whether the rock was worn down from the constant and consistent battering and finally broke due to the cumulative impact of all the hits. Whatever way you think, you must make the commitment that you will not stop, that you will not give up, that you will not give in. "Don't *stop!*" The main thing is that the rock, the obstacle in your way, finally broke and is no longer in your way! Don't *stop!*

Next is *thinking*. Keep thinking up new ideas and new ways to turn this setback into a comeback. Keep thinking! Napoleon Hill wrote that we must "Think and Grow Rich!" If you keep thinking and keep allowing your mind to soar and explore new options, you will be amazed at what you come up with to achieve your goals. I believe that problems are not really money problems but rather idea problems. It's time to come up with some new ideas and some new thinking. Albert Einstein once said (in the book, *Bite-Size Einstein*, Gramercy Publishing, 2003) that the thinking that got you this far will not get you to the next level. So we must continue to think up! We need to think bigger, bolder, and better! We must continue to push the envelope and come up with new ideas. If one idea doesn't work, come up with another idea. Keep thinking about the future and all the incredible opportunities that are within our grasp. Don't stop *thinking* about tomorrow.

The next word that we will emphasize is the word *about*. When we emphasize this word, we come to the realization that there are tremendous opportunities all about, all around us! Is it a tough market? Yes! Is it a tough economic landscape? Yes! Is it going to be hard? Yes! But the truth is that business is challenging even in good times; it is just more challenging now. So this is the time when we develop the muscle that will fuel the fire when we get back to a good economy. Another part of thinking *about* the possibilities is to remember the last time we were in a tough economic situation. What did we do then? Remember what we did to get through that experience, and just do it again, but do more of it! Think back and remind yourself of past successes and past experiences. I often think about my first summer as a speaker. I was brand new, didn't know anyone, and didn't know much about the speaking business. I had been speaking at schools during the school year, but when the school year ended in June, I didn't have any work and therefore didn't have any money. I was definitely in an economic downturn. I didn't know how I was going to pay my mortgage or my bills, so I got on the phone and literally went through the *Yellow Pages* asking people if they had a need for a speaker. I finally got two small contracts—one to speak for a youth arts camp and the other to be a part-time speaker/counselor for a small community-based youth theatrical group. Somehow, I made it through the summer and paid my bills. Once school started again, I got calls from some of the administrators who had worked with the two programs during the summer; they booked me in their individual schools and helped me get bookings at their brother and sister schools. I made it through. Over the years, whenever I have had times that were tight financially, I think about that summer and how I got through those times by faith, focus, and follow-through. Because I made it through at that time, it has been easier for me to sleep at night other times when finances got tight, because I remember that when I didn't know anyone and didn't know much about speaking, I refused to quit and I made it then . . . and I will make it now! Remind yourself about the successes of the past and use them to empower you as you go forward into the future.

The last part of this phrase is the word *tomorrow*. In the hit movie and Broadway play *Annie*, the star of the show, an orphan girl named Annie, sings a song called "Tomorrow." In the song, she proclaims that the sun will come out tomorrow— that you can depend on the fact that tomorrow, there will be sun. And if you think about those bright tomorrows, it will take away all the tears, the pain, and the sorrow. The tears of today will be replaced by the smiles of tomorrow.

Don't Give Up

Don't Quit! Keep Looking Up! Because if you can look up you can get up!

—*Les Brown*

This sounds elementary and simple, but for some reason when tough times come around, people seem to forget that they must not give up. This is an absolute necessity for turning your situation around, and for turning your setbacks into greenbacks. You simply cannot give up!

You would think this would be something that we could not forget, because every motivational book I have ever read has had some information about the power of perseverance and persistence. In tough times, though, we seem to forget this important ingredient in the success formula.

Why do people forget such an important ingredient? Sometimes people forget because the massive amount of bad news that floods the marketplace overwhelms them. Sometimes they forget because they have taken their eyes off their dreams and goals and started to focus on their problems. As I learned years ago, when you take your eyes off your possibilities and look at your problems and circumstances, you start to suffer.

There is a great example of this in the Bible. Jesus was walking on the water, and Peter stepped out of the boat and walked on the water toward Jesus. Peter was fine as long as he kept his eyes on Jesus, but as soon as he looked down and saw the water, he started to sink.

A more recent example is Bob Wieland, the legless marathon runner. Bob was an all-star athlete well on his way to becoming a professional baseball player when he was drafted to serve in Vietnam. While in battle, one of his comrades was hit and Bob went to rescue him. While trying to bring his friend to safety, Bob was hit with a mortar round and lost both of his legs. Rather than dwelling on his lost baseball career or on losing his ability to walk and run, Bob Wieland chose to focus on the challenges that were ahead. He decided to take on the challenge of running a marathon—26 miles—without legs. He would go the 26 miles by placing his hands on the ground and swinging his body forward. Each "step" involved swinging his body with his hands. When he ran his first marathon, it took many days. By the time he finished, his hands were raw and bloodied. The pain was intense, yet when a newspaper reporter asked him how he handled the intense pain, he responded that the only time he felt it was when he took his eyes off the goal!

When you start focusing on your possibilities instead of your problems, you will find that life becomes much more manageable. A wide array of positive possibilities are available to you, but you must decide whether to focus on your problems or your possibilities. Those who focus on their problems without thinking about solutions or coming up with positive possibilities are those who are destined to just survive, not thrive, in the midst of the tough times. Instead, focus on the fact that you have life, and that you live in a time and place where success actually can be achieved. How do I know this is true? I know because history has taught that some of the greatest businesses were born in the midst of tough times. IBM, Hewlett-Packard, Microsoft, Disney, and Wal-Mart are all examples of this. And some of the wealthiest people in the world started building their wealth in the midst of tough economic times.

Those who win over the long term are those who decide to focus on the good news rather than the bad news. (That is one of the reasons I recently started a new organization called Jolley Good News to help people get positive news, rather than a constant diet of negative news. Visit www.jolley-goodnews.org for more information on this organization and how it can help you to grow and succeed at the next level.)

I believe you must make a commitment to fill yourself with the pure, the powerful, and the positive. I believe that we should have a reservoir from which to draw inspiration and motivation. I believe that we should dig our wells before we are thirsty and start reading and listening to positive information before we need it. During tough times, people seem to forget the basics and resort to the old ways of focusing on the bad news that comes from the news media. The news media consistently make a habit of looking at life through a negative lens. If the sun is halfway shining, they will say "partly cloudy" rather than "partly sunny!" The old adage for the news is "If it bleeds, it leads!"

Sometimes people forget the basic principle of not giving up, because they have been influenced by their negative, small-minded friends and family members. If you are going to turn your setbacks into greenbacks, it is critical that you surround yourself with positive people. I often talk about *dream-busters*—those who lurk around and make it their job to kill dreams. Unfortunately, these are often people in our inner circles. They are people we love, and people who actually love us; they are not trying to be mean-spirited when they crush your hopes and dreams and tell you they are just trying to be real! They just happen to suffer from *possibility blindness*. They say they are trying to be real, and figure that because times are tough you should just lie down and die—all while the winners are pushing forward and seeing opportunity and possibility.

The dreams of tomorrow can focus our actions today. Stephen Covey says, "The most effective people always start with the end in mind, then they move towards that picture!" To turn your setbacks into greenbacks, you must keep thinking about the future and how things can get better.

This is a song that was on my *Money Making Music and Motivation* CD that speaks about the power of being motivated.

HIGHLY MOTIVATED!

Written By Willie Jolley and Paul Minor

Motivated, highly motivated, motivated, gonna take
  it to the top
Motivated, highly motivated, motivated, I'm never
  gonna stop

Verse 1:
I had a job, a job I really hated
It made me sick, but it got me motivated
I knew this was not where I was meant to be

I didn't want to stay but I was too afraid to leave
But then one day I got my check and there was
    almost nothing there
I went to the boss; he laughed and said he didn't
    care
My kids were at home hungry; I was about to lose
    my home
That's when I decided I had to make it on my own

Chorus:
Motivated, highly motivated, motivated, gonna take
    it to the top
Motivated, highly motivated, motivated, I'm never
    gonna stop

Verse 2:
My friends said I was crazy when I told them all
    goodbye
But the only one who's crazy is the one who's
    afraid to try
They said I wouldn't make it, said I would not
    survive
But I knew I had to make it, it was either do or die
So I grabbed hold of my dream and I put it in my
    heart
I stepped out on my faith and learned to really trust
    in God
I knew I had to fight, fight with all my power
Then things started happening, blessings came, oh
    hour after hour

Chorus:
Motivated, highly motivated, motivated, gonna take
    it to the top

Motivated, highly motivated, motivated, I'm never
    gonna stop
I found that dreams do come true, if you believe,
Believe in you
Don't worry about what others say
If you're serious you'll make a way

Spoken Word 1:
Hannibal said, "If you cannot find a way, then
    make a way!"
See it doesn't matter so much what happens around
    you, or to you
What matters is what happens in you!
When people stomp on your dreams
Don't get mad! Don't get even!
Get Ahead! Because massive success is the best
    revenge!

Verse 3:
So when people laugh at you and they try to put
    you down
Take that negative and turn it all around!
Grab hold of your dream, let it set your soul on fire
Activate your faith and take it higher, higher!
Yeah, going to take it to the top!
I'm never going to stop
If you've got faith, God's got the power
To bless your life, hour after hour
Keep the faith, keep the desire
Keep reaching up, until you reach the sky!
Never going to stop believing what I can do
I've got the power, you can have it too
Start with the dream, add the desire

Don't Stop Thinking and Dreaming

Turn on your faith, and take it higher
Take it to the top! Yeah!

Spoken Word 2:
Someone said in life, "You've got to Pray, like it all
    depends on God
And Work like it all depends on You!"
Folks, it's time to get Motivated . . . Highly
    Motivated!
It's time to Live Your Dreams!

As I thought about the steps I had used to turn my economic setback into a comeback, I realized that one of the first steps is to make the commitment to not stop trying. This is a concept that is as old as time. In every success manual I have in my library (and there are thousands), I have seen the statement over and over again, that you must persist and persevere. Yet as I learned more about success, I realized that persistence and perseverance are actually quite different. To persist means to keep going after your goal in an obstinate, repetitive way. To keep hitting, keep fighting, and keep working on your goal until you achieve it. Thomas Edison was persistent; he failed more than a thousand times in his quest to invent a light bulb, yet he refused to give up, and ultimately achieved his goal. I like to say that "persistence breaks down resistance!"

To persevere is to cultivate the attitude that somehow, some way, you will get through the tough times and get to a better place in your life. You will make up your mind that you will be the last person standing. I like the cartoon of the little frog that is holding onto a rope that has a knot in it; the caption reads, "When you get to the end of your rope, tie a knot and hold on!"

It is important that you persist and persevere in tough time to achieve your goals and turn your economic setbacks into greenbacks. It is common to implore people to persist and persevere, but it is uncommon to see people actually taking this advice to heart and doing it. Statistics show that most people do not achieve their goals and dreams, because they simply give up. And I have seen many people give up when they are within striking distance of their goal. I have a family member who worked hard to develop a team for her network marketing company; when she got her first check, it was less than she had expected and she got angry and quit; not realizing that all rivers start with a drip of water. I can remember when I started writing books. Initially, I was just making a few pennies per book, yet as more people started talking about the books and telling their friends, my pennies turned into dimes, then quarters, then dollars, all because I did not stop! Don't stop trying! Don't quit! Don't give up!

Believe in the Power of Your Dreams

Dreams are the seeds for success. You have to have a dream. Every single success story I have ever read or heard about talks about the power of dreams. Scripture says without a vision the people perish—yet what goes unsaid is that "with a vision a people will flourish!" You must have a vision! You must have a dream, a goal of what is possible in the future, and not solely dwell on what is going on today. Dreams and goals give us hope for the future and give us the will to keep going, in spite of present problems. We all know about the power of dreams and goals for helping us to focus and get a game plan, yet I want to say that we need dreams and goals in tough times as well, because they give us hope for the journey.

There is power in our dreams; we should hold fast to them and let them empower us to achieve. An exciting new movie called *The Opus* (www .theopusmovie.com) is making its way around the world. It is a follow-up to the hit movie *The Secret*, but with a different perspective. *The Opus* talks about the fact that success is the result of a process. The process involves vision (the power of a dream), planning (the power of preparation), and performance (the power of taking action and making the dream into a reality). Like *The Secret*, *The Opus* features selected experts who give teaching points throughout the movie, yet it also has a Disney-like story interwoven through the messages from the experts. I was honored to be asked to be one of the experts, and in one of my messages, I share my favorite story about the power of dreams.

It was a hot summer day in the summer of 1944, on the campus of Morehouse College in Atlanta, Georgia. The esteemed president of the college, Dr. Benjamin Mays, was sitting in his office; he was a dignified man with gray hair, wearing a suit and dabbing perspiration from his brow.

There was a knock on the door. Dr. Mays said, "Come in," and the big, wooden door swung open to show a man and a teenage boy. Dr. Mays jumped to his feet and moved quickly to grab the hand of the man, his old friend, Reverend Martin Luther King, Sr.—Daddy King.

"Come in, my friend!" Dr. Mays proclaimed.

Daddy King stepped in and said, "Dr. Mays, I know you are busy, so I won't take a lot of your time. I just came by to introduce you to my son M. L. His real name is Martin Luther King, Jr., but we call him M. L. He is 15 years old and just graduated from high school. He is going to college here in the fall and I need a big favor." Daddy King continued, "I don't need help with tuition or room and board; what I need is bigger! This boy has something special inside of him, I can just sense it, and I

87

Don't Stop Thinking and Dreaming

want to ask if you would teach him how to dream! Would you teach my son how to dream big dreams?"

Dr. Mays handed young M. L. a piece of paper and told him to read it daily. On the paper, Dr. Mays had written:

It must be borne in mind that the tragedy of life does not lie in not reaching your goal. The tragedy lies in not having a goal to reach for! It is not a calamity to die with your dreams unfulfilled, but it is a calamity not to dream. It is not a disaster to be unable to capture your ideal, but it is a disaster to have no ideals to capture. It is not a disgrace not to reach the stars, but it is a disgrace to have no stars to reach for. Not failure, but low aim is sin!

Friends, I implore you to dream big dreams! I love the quote of a father who said to his son, "Dream dreams that are so big that you cannot achieve them in one lifetime."

What are your goals? What are your dreams? Everything you use today started in someone's mind. It started as a thought and went on to become a manifestation of the thought. Success always starts on the inside and then manifests itself on the outside. As Dennis Kimbro, author of *What*

Makes the Great Great, shared when I interviewed him, "First is the thought, then create the thing. First is the inner, which creates the outer!" If the dream is big enough, the problems don't matter.

How to Set Goals that Get You Going

Scripture says, write the vision, make it plain, that he that reads it may run the race! You need to have written dreams and goals and read them regularly to keep you focused on where you want to go and what you want to achieve. The reason I don't make New Year's resolutions is that they typically are not written and are usually forgotten by the end of January. Yet goals that are written give you power! If you want to create wealth, it is important that you write down your dreams and goals and read them regularly.

One additional step to creating wealth is to determine *why* you want to hit your goals. First you need a goal, but if you are really serious you will take the next step and find compelling reasons to keep going until you achieve the goal. These reasons will empower you and keep you focused when distractions come into play. Maybe your reason to become wealthy is to be able to buy your parents a home, or to be able give your children a better life than you had, or maybe it is because someone was kind to you when you were down and out and you want to repay that kindness by helping others. I don't know what your reasons may be, but I do know that people who have compelling reasons to reach their goals tend to achieve those goals more quickly and more fully than other people. It is good to want to create wealth, but if you can identify a compelling reason for doing so, it will have a powerful impact on your success! Do you have goals? Are they written? What are your reasons? What are your why's? I recommend you answer these questions right now, and then take the necessary steps to start making these dreams and goals into realities. Neitzsche said, "If you know the why of living, you can endure any how!" Make a decision to find your why!

I also want to share a technique I have used with some of my coaching clients when they have struggled to find their reason and have struggled to get compelling why's. I know that we all enjoy receiving unexpected presents, but I also have found that people love to see the expression on the faces of their loved ones when they give those people presents. Even the coldest, coolest people get some satisfaction from the impact of their giving. So I started working with my clients on four categories to help them structure their goals. First I ask them to write their "Giving Goals." What would they like to give? What legacy would they like to leave? What impact would they like to have on the lives of others?

Next I help them understand that in order to "Give," they must first "Get," because you cannot give what you do not have! So I ask them to write their "Getting Goals." What do you need to get—what do you need to generate in order to give the things you would like to give? It is amazing that when we tie the getting to giving, it takes on more intensity than when we just want to get for ourselves. I have found that most parents will do more for their children than they will do for themselves. They have things that they personally want, but they will tend to do for their children first, then do for themselves. That is why it is good to know what our giving goals are before we work on our getting goals. What must you "Get" in order that you can "Give?"

The next category is the "Doing Goals." What must you "Do" in order that you can "Get" so that you can "Give?" This is when you start to map out your daily activities for generating more income. What steps must you take and what plans must you make? What must you do, and what things must you stop doing, to achieve your goals? We all have things in our lives that we do that are counterproductive to us reaching our goals. (An example was when I said I wanted to lose some weight, yet I was eating ice cream at night . . . it was

91

Don't Stop Thinking and Dreaming

counterproductive to my goal, so I had to stop!) Three major questions that you must ask yourself . . . what are you doing, what more could you do, and what things must you stop doing to achieve your goals? Once you know what you must do and what you must stop doing, you are on your way to greater success and you will be clear what you must do in order for you to get, so that you can give!

Finally, what are your "Be Goals?" What must you be, so that you can do, so that you can get, so that you can give? To do something you have never done, you must become someone you have never been! What must you become to be the person who can navigate the challenging economic seas and create greater wealth? What do you need to learn in regards to financial literacy? What books on business do you need to read? What new skill sets must you develop? What new habits must you cultivate? Who must you become in order to be the person who can achieve incredible results? I believe we all have potential that is not yet tapped, and if we start to tap into that potential we will amaze ourselves. Emerson said, "That which is before us and that which is behind can never compare with that which is within us!" In the movie *The Lion King*, Mufasa says to his son, Simba, "My son, you are more than what you have become!"

Turn Setbacks into Greenbacks

I believe that there is more in us than we even know, yet we must be willing to constantly grow ourselves and develop ourselves. If we want greater results, we must be better; therefore, I am now learning Spanish and French so I can communicate with more people. I am exploring ways that I can continue to grow, and I implore you to continue to grow yourself and continue to develop yourself! What must you "Be", so that you can "Do", so that you can "Get", so that you can "Give?" I truly believe that if you answer these questions you will see that your future will become clearer and much brighter!

STEP 5

Be Proactive

> Your future depends on many things, but mostly on you!
>
> —*Frank Tyger*

To turn your finances around, it is critical that you become proactive. The word *proactive* was popularized by Dr. Stephen Covey in his book, *The 7 Habits of Highly Effective People.* I first read his book years ago, but last year I had the opportunity to speak at the same conference with him in Australia, and we developed a friendship. I was able to learn in greater depth what he meant by *proactive.* To be proactive is to take anticipatory actions. Dr. Covey felt that all of his seven habits were important but that being proactive was the bedrock habit—the foundation from which the other habits spring forth.

To be proactive is to recognize that your personal actions can have an impact on your present situation and change it for the better. Being proactive means you take action instead of just sitting and waiting. Being proactive means you are "being up and doing" (as my mother used to say about people who were ambitious). Being proactive means taking responsibility for your future and being willing to move on your thoughts and dreams rather than waiting for them to manifest. You take the necessary actions to make those thoughts and dreams into realities, and think through what the necessary steps will require.

Being proactive is the opposite of being *reactive*, which means to wait for some outside stimulus to appear in order for things to change. Reactive people have a mind-set that "this is just the way things are, and we cannot do anything to change them." Proactive people do not wait for things to happen—they make things happen! To turn your economic setbacks into greenbacks, it is necessary that you be proactive.

Winners Make Things Happen, Losers Let Things Happen

On my desk is a sign that states: "Winners make things happen, losers let things happen!" Some people state it a little differently; they say, "Some people make things happen, other people watch what happened, and then the rest stand around and ask, 'What happened?'" Whatever way you want to say it, the truth remains that winners are those who make a determined decision to make things happen! When asked what keeps them from being successful, most people will blame the government, or the economy, or their families, or the "isms" of life (you know . . . sexism, racism, ageism, etc.). But the one thing that most people avoid in their list is that which is most important. It is the person we see every day in the mirror . . . it is us! We are the main obstacles to our success in life!

It has been stated, and I believe it is true, that success follows the 80/20 rule: 80 percent of the work usually comes from 20 percent of the people. In personal achievement, this means we are responsible for 80 percent of our failure to hit our goals, and outside obstacles are only 20 percent of the problem. The old African proverb states, "If you can overcome the enemy on the inside, the enemy on the outside can do you no harm!" We must be brutally honest with ourselves and come to the realization that we are the biggest challenge to our own success!

If you want to win, you must stop letting things happen and start making things happen. Remember, when all is said and done, much more is said than done . . . so let's go get it done! Today, make a commitment to overcome yourself, so you can reach your goals.

During tough economic times, some people sit and wait for the economy to change. They talk about how bad things are, and they just want to survive the storms. Yet there are others who do not wait for things to happen, they make things happen. Michael V. Roberts is one of those people. In fact, he has made things happen so successfully that he and his brother, Steven, now run a number of companies under the Roberts & Roberts banner that have a combined worth of almost $2 billion. He is a man who realizes that tough economic situations present big challenges, but also offer big opportunities.

I met Mike Roberts when I spoke at the A. G. Gaston Economic Conference in Birmingham, Alabama. He was the opening speaker and I was the luncheon speaker, so I came down early to listen to his message. As I sat and listened to his story, I was totally blown away.

He shared how he had grown up in the inner city of St. Louis, Missouri, with working-class parents "who were not poor, but just never had any money." He went to college and law school, and when he finished law school he saw that St. Louis was in the midst of economic calamity. Many of the big industrial companies had shut down, and many of the houses were abandoned and boarded up. He started a small development company with his brother and also started working on changing the mental attitude of the citizens of the city. He was so successful that he was elected to the city council. Soon thereafter, his brother was elected to the city council as well. They kept working on projects to improve the city and eventually their company grew so large that they had to commit all of their time to the company. They left the city council and started working on building more and more housing for the citizens of St. Louis.

The Roberts brothers expanded their business to include a construction company and then a media company, when they were able to buy a small television station. They continued to grow both businesses and became one of the biggest developers and media companies in the country. They now own hotels around the United States, telecom companies, and airplane leasing services—and all because they used a down and depressed economic situation to build a tremendous business. Mike has written a book, *Action Has No Season,* which focuses on the fact that those who are proactive do not care about the time but know that there are always opportunities for those who are committed and determined to be successful. In the book, he has invented a new word, *actionaire,* which refers to people who do not wait for things to happen, but rather take action and make things happen! Mike Roberts says that if you want to create wealth you must be willing to learn as much as you can about your particular business and then learn as much as you can about running a business and managing people and performance. He encourages people in his book to pursue wealth and not simply try to become "rich." He says that rich people tend to think in terms of one generation, while wealthy people think in terms of legacy, meaning that their wealth can be maintained and sustained over many generations.

He says that rich people scream, while wealthy people whisper. He says that rich people tend to look and act like they are rich and stand out as being rich, while wealthy people tend to be understated in their wealth. And I think Mike is on to something because in the Bible, God tends to frown on being rich (the story of the rich young ruler, and the parable of it being harder for a rich man to get into heaven than it is for a camel to go through the eye of a needle). Yet God tends to smile on being wealthy! (Deut 8:18, it is God who gives you the power to get wealth; Proverbs 13:22, A good man leaves an inheritance for his children, but the wealth of the sinner is stored up for the righteous).

Mike also says that when he and his brother started they didn't have two dimes to rub together. They did not come from a wealthy family, but although they did not have much money, they had a dream and a willingness to work hard and invest the time and energy to get up and going. The Roberts brothers both agree that there will be challenges and setbacks, but you must keep a positive outlook and make up your mind that you are in it to win it! Start with a dream, work hard on your plan, and then take massive action! Be an actionaire and play to win!

To Be Proactive Means to Get Up and Take Action!

If you are going to turn your setback into green-backs, then it is absolutely necessary that you take action. Jack Canfield, the co-author of the best selling *Chicken Soup for the Soul* series, shared with me that he and his co-author Mark Victor Hanson got turned down by over 30 publishers, but they kept believing in their book and, there-fore, they kept trying. Finally a small publisher (Health Communications, Inc.,) took a chance on them and signed them to a publishing deal. HCI could not give them a big advance and could not promise massive distribution. They told HCI if it would just get the books into stores, then they would do the work to get the books out of the stores. They would hustle and work 24/7 to pro-mote the books. They went to work and made a commitment to do two radio or television inter-views each and every day. They did this for over a year, and slowly but surely the books started to sell. Within a few years, they had a national bestseller, then an international bestseller, and then a second portion of Chicken Soup came out and it too became a bestseller. And from there a multimillion dollar success story unfolded for Mark and Jack. You have to be proactive and take action.

Jack shared an example of how he shares the importance of being proactive with his audience. After talking about his challenges with creating his own successful story and how he had to get up and take action, he pulls out a $100 bill, and says, "Who wants this $100 bill!" People wave their hands and holler and scream at him but he just holds the bill . . . . until someone gets up out of their seat and comes up to the front of the room and takes it out of his hand! That is the person who wins!

Author and Success Coach, John Di Lemme says:

The winner—is always part of the answer.

The loser—is always part of the problem.

The winner—sees an answer for every problem.

The loser—sees a problem for every answer.

The winner—sees a green near every sand trap.

The loser—sees two or three sand traps near every green.

The winner—says "It may be difficult, but it's possible!"

Turn Setbacks into Greenbacks

The loser—says "It may be possible, but it's too difficult!"

The winner—says "I must do something!"

The loser—says—"Something must be done!"

Choose to be a winner!

Get Up and Get Going—Find Your Good Foot and Get on It!

James Brown had a popular song when I was young that went, "Get up on the good foot . . . everybody get up!" As we look at the process of creating wealth, I think it is a good idiom from which to draw a conclusion about your success and wealth building. First, if you are serious about your success you must make a commitment to *get up and get going.* Very little success comes to you unless you are involved in the process. Author Bo Bennett says in his collection of quotes (*Years to Success*, Archieboy Holdings LLC, 2004), "Confusing the words hope, wish, faith, and pray with each other usually just results in a minor grammatical faux pas, but when any of these words, especially hope, are confused with action, the results can be devastating!" The Scripture says (in James 2:26 NKJV) that faith without works is dead. You must get up and take action on your goals and dreams!

Everybody has a good foot, the skill or gift with which they have been blessed. You must find your gift and be willing to use it. Dennis Kimbro says that one of the keys to success and wealth building is to find your competitive advantage and exploit it. He said to imagine a 7-foot, 300-pound guy who decides to become a jockey because someone told him that was an option. It sounds silly, but every day we find people who listen to others about their future and never find or recognize their own natural gifts. Some people are good with art, others might be good with writing, others might be good with organization or analysis, and others might be good with cooking. I don't know what your "good foot" is, but I do know that everyone has something that comes easily to them. I recommend you find your good foot, get up on it, and get busy!

Let me say that occasionally life will throw you a curveball and take away that "good foot" option. For instance, maybe your company downsized or eliminated your position, and you are unable to find work. If for some reason you cannot get up on your good foot, I say get up on whatever foot you can until you can do better. As my friend Walter Bond, the former professional basketball player who was recently named Speaker of the Year by the Minnesota Tourism Association, says, "I got fired from basketball and realized I had to find a new love. So I went to work on me and found that I had other gifts and skills that I simply needed to work on and develop." I say, if you cannot get up on your good foot, get up on whatever foot you can get up on and get busy!

Dr. Covey popularized the word *proactive*, but it is not a new concept. People throughout history have found that taking action can have tremendous benefits. They just called it by different names. As I said earlier, my mother called it "being up and doing." Other phrases I have heard since childhood are "go-getter" and a "make-it-happen person." All these terms describe the same idea: to change your present circumstances, you must take action and work hard. I like to say that you've got to hustle!

Understanding the Power of Hustle

In terms of turning your setbacks into greenbacks, you must be willing to hustle. You decide to consistently work on your hustle muscle and develop it and make it stronger. As with any other muscle, the way to grow your hustle muscle is to exercise it, because the more you work the muscle, the stronger it gets. Just as if you wanted to grow your biceps you would exercise those muscles, so too must you exercise your hustle muscle. Develop it, strengthen it, and make it a muscle that works for you, because you have made the decision to work on it.

I made a commitment to hustle when I started my speaking business, and have continued to hustle since day one. My friend James Carter, the Unstoppable Visionary, was a guest on my radio show and said, "Some people have a sales plan and a marketing plan, but very few have a hustle plan! Willie Jolley taught me the power of having a hustle plan!"

You might ask, what is a hustle plan? It is simply a determination that you will work harder than others think is necessary. You will do what is necessary to reach your goals, as long as it is moral and legal. You will not give up or give in until you achieve your goal. You will fight and keep fighting for your dreams!

I love what Bishop T. D. Jakes said about the power of hustle. He said that many people wonder where he came from and how he seemed to pop onto the scene. People do not realize that he struggled and scraped for 25 years in the back hills of West Virginia in order to become an "overnight" success. He said that he dug ditches to support his family while he was working on his craft, and preached to conferences where there were 25 people in the audience. He traveled around in an old, beat-up car, yet he refused to give up and continued to hustle. He said that when he dies, he recommends that you look under his fingernails, because you will find dirt there. Why? Because he never stopped scraping and clawing, even when he became famous.

I say that you must get a hustle plan, and it will take you places you never imagined you would go. Never forget the bridge that brings you across; it usually is the bridge that takes you to the next level.

Once I went to the National Association of College Activities Convention. They were choosing the speakers for the year. I could not afford the registration fee for the convention, so I called a friend who was starting to get some speeches at colleges, and I asked him to let me stay in his room.

Since I couldn't afford the registration, I went to the convention hall and I stood outside and gave out my little flyers about my speaking business. When my friend saw me, he told me "Stop, man. That is not cool or sophisticated; it's embarrassing!" As soon as he left, I started giving out the flyers again. When he saw me again, he was angry. He said, "Man, this is not how we do it. You are embarrassing yourself!" Yet, again as soon as he left, I started back up and continued until I had given out all my flyers.

Later that day, I was walking near the convention center, and a man started hollering out to me. I thought he was security and might have been upset because I had broken the rules and handed out my flyers outside the convention hall, but I decided to just deal with whatever he had to say. The man caught up with me and said, "Are you the guy who was giving out those flyers this morning?" I said, "Yes, I confess . . . it was me!" He said, "Good! I have been looking for you all day! I am the owner of the biggest college booking agency, and I think that if you have enough guts to hustle and work like you did today, then I think you will be a help to our agency." He went on to become my biggest booking agent for colleges! This happened because I was willing to hustle.

Abraham Lincoln said, "Things may come to those who wait, but only things left behind by those who hustle." I say, "Good things come to those who wait, but you have to hustle if you want to be *great*!" To create a growing business, you have to hustle! So go get busy . . . and hustle!

Be Aggressive!

When I was in high school, there was a cheer that we would all shout when our team was down and we wanted to fire them up. The cheerleaders would lead the cheer and then we would all join and shout it at the top of our lungs: *Be Aggressive!*

Be Aggressive! B-E A-G-G-R-E-S-S-I-V-E! Be Aggressive! Be Aggressive! The chant would continue until our team responded, played harder, and turned the game around. In basketball, there is a defense that is often utilized when a team is down and trying to turn the game around. It is called a "full court press." It is a tactic used when the defense is super aggressive and has made the decision that they will no longer let things happen, but will instead make things happen. Similarly, if you are going to turn your setbacks into greenbacks, you will have to be aggressive!

Learn to Love Sales and Marketing

The next point of interest for turning your setbacks into greenbacks is to be more active in getting more people to know about you. It is critical for you to market, market, market, and sell, sell, sell. The old adage states, "Nothing happens until a sale is made!" You must be willing to sell your thoughts and ideas. Sell your products and services, and convince the marketplace that you have something of interest that can benefit them. I tell my staff that it is important to realize that people have pain and difficulty all around them, and our job is to sell them an aspirin to ease that pain. As noted consultant Jim Feldman said on my XM Radio program, "you must first see the need, then fill the need, then charge for supplying the solution." The key to it all is the willingness to talk to people and sell them on your solution. You have to learn to love to sell if you are serious about turning your setbacks into greenbacks!

A speaker friend called one day, and during the conversation he said, "You know, I love speaking, but right now we are having difficulty with our sales. I hate selling!" As soon as he said it, I knew why his sales were suffering. I told him, "If you ever want to have success in your life, you must sell. Therefore, you can never let those words come out of your mouth again. In fact, you can never let those words enter your thoughts! To have success, you must learn to sell your ideas, your products, or your services. And to sell them effectively, you have to learn to love selling!"

I told my speaker friend that I had learned a valuable lesson years ago, when I had just started traveling and speaking around the country. I was getting some name recognition, and I was receiving invitations to speak all across the United States, so I was getting on and off planes every day. The travel was fun at first, but after about a year the traveling lost its glamour, and I started to dread it.

About that time, I had a conversation with another speaker friend, Keith Harrell, the author of *Attitude Is Everything*, who was also traveling a lot. I said, "Man, I hate this travel!" He said, "Willie you can never let those words come out of your mouth again, because whatever you speak eventually becomes your reality."

Keith then asked me a very poignant question; "Willie, what do you love to do?"

I replied, "I love to speak and inspire people."

He then said, "Do you agree that in order to do what you love, you might have to travel occasionally, and that perhaps that really is the price you have to pay in order to do what you love?"

"Well . . . yes, I suppose that is true," I admitted.

Keith said, "Then you can never ever say again that you hate to travel, because travel is really just a price you pay to get to do what you love to do!"

I shared that story with my friend who had said, "I hate selling," and told him that he had to think differently. I told him that when I was in college, I took a logic class and I learned about deductive logic, which states that if Socrates is a man, and all men are mortal, then Socrates must be mortal. Going along the same line of thinking, if he loved to speak (which he told me he loved to do), and if selling was what he must do in order to speak more, then logic would say that therefore he loved selling!

He was quiet for a few seconds and said, "You know what, Willie . . . you are right!" He then proclaimed, "I love selling! I love selling! I love selling!" His sales started to improve, because his thinking improved and his attitude improved.

One of the points I share with audiences is that they must TTP: "Talk to people." When I got started speaking, I had a five-foot rule: If someone was within five feet of me, I was going to talk to them and tell them about my business. I remember a time when I stood at the subway in Washington, D.C. and gave out my little "ugly" flyers. I call the flyers "ugly" because they were not fancy or profession-ally reproduced, but they were the best I could do at the moment. So I went with what I had to work with, because it was critical that I get my business going, and I needed to get it going quickly.

I stood at the subway and handed out those ugly little flyers. Some people looked at the flyers and then ditched them in the trash, but some took them and read them. A few weeks later, I got a call from a government agency and the woman on the phone booked me to speak for her organization. I asked her how she had heard about me, and she said that someone on her team had taken a flyer at the subway, and when they were looking for a speaker, they decided to use me. I believe that you must make a commitment to TTP. Let people know who you are and what you can do to bring value to the marketplace. Once you TTP, I recom-mend you TTMP—talk to more people!

One of the marketing techniques I have used over the years is a technique I learned from one of my mentors, Joe Charbonneau. Joe was one of the early sales coaches in the speaking business, and he taught a sales technique called *13, 13, 12, & 12*. He said that if you made 13 sales calls on Monday and 13 on Tuesday, then followed that up with 12 sales calls on Wednesday and another 12 on Thursday, and then sent out correspondence to all of those people on Friday, then you would have made 50 new sales contacts that week. It sounds so elementary that I wondered if it was enough, but when I actually got 13 conversations in a day, followed by 13 conversations on the second day and then 12 conversations followed by 12 more conversations, it was amazing how my business started to grow. I realized it was not just the fact that I was making the calls, but also that I was using a system. And many people have become millionaires because they followed a prescribed system for success—just as many people are able to lose weight on specific diet systems when they couldn't do it on their own. And the same is true for creating wealth: Find a sales system that works, and follow it!

Another one of my buddies and frequent guests on my XM show is Larry Winget, television personality and *New York Times* best-selling author. Larry has been featured in a number of television

Be Proactive

shows, including *Big Spender* on the A&E network and on television commercials for Hyundai, and he was one of the first people I met when I started my speaking career. We immediately connected because we are similarly focused on marketing as a main way to build our brands and our income. Larry says that there are two, and only two, reasons why your business is not prospering. First, your product or service is not good enough, so you should continue to improve your product or service. Two, you are not marketing to enough people. You are not talking to enough people who can purchase your product or service. I agree with Larry that you need a good product, and then you have to make a commitment to get the word out. You must talk to a lot of people or use technology to help you get your business's message to a lot of people. One thing for sure is that people cannot buy from you if they do not know you exist!

To Be Outstanding You Must Stand Out!

If you are serious about becoming wealthy, you must stand out from the crowd and out-work and out-think your competition. Make a commitment to be distinct and build your brand. Best-selling author and speaker Scott McKain was a guest on my show and said that you just need to be 1 percent better than your competitor. Just commit to do a little more than your competition. Give a little more, go a little further, and try a little harder. Remember, the horse that wins the Kentucky Derby by a nose makes 10 times as much as the horse that takes second place. Set yourself apart . . . get up, get busy, and hustle.

While I was speaking in Okinawa, Japan, for the U.S. Marines, a group of Marines took me out to dinner one evening, and I saw a lot of bright neon signs. I asked about the places that had the bright signs, and I was told that those businesses were the casinos, and the bright lights were there to attract customers. My host said, "You know the bright neon lights attract customers just like lanterns attract bugs!"

Over the next few days, I noticed that the casinos did not only have bright lights, but they also had lots of signs and advertisements all around the island. And from what I was told, these businesses saw rapid growth once they started advertising. I realized there was a lesson in this action . . . that the businesses that grow most rapidly are those that understand the power of standing out!

In order to have an "outstanding business," you need to "stand out" from the crowd. Whether it's a casino with bright lights or a small business with a big ad in the newspaper, those businesses that

117

grow most rapidly are those that understand the power of getting the word out about their organization! I have found a truism that applies here: it is hard to grow your business if no one knows you are in business.

If people don't know you are in business, they cannot call and therefore they cannot do business with you. Many people are working hard to grow their businesses but are missing a valuable tool for that job, which is advertising. I like what Ted Turner said about the secret to his business success. "Early to bed and early to rise . . . work like crazy and advertise!" Folks, I recommend you make a commitment to take advantage of the powerful business growth tool called advertising! The old adage is true: A business with no sign usually is a sign of no business! Do not be ashamed to let people know you are in business.

The Paradox of Risks and Rewards

Why is it that most people do not maximize their potential? The answer is fear! Fear is the number one reason people do not act on their thoughts and dreams. Fear will stop people in their tracks and make them stop trying. We must overcome our fears, or our fears will definitely overcome us.

You must take risks if you are going to turn your setbacks into greenbacks. The challenge is, what risk are you going to take? I have a few ideas that can help you manage risk. A few years ago, I was invited to speak at High Point University in High Point, North Carolina, where my friend Nido Qubein is the president. Nido is not only the president of High Point University but also one of America's foremost business development experts. He is an award-winning speaker, a best-selling author, and a master businessman. If you are not familiar with Nido, I recommend you visit his web site, www.nidoqubein.com. While visiting with Nido, I asked him about the secret to his amazing success.

He said, "Brother Willie, the key is to understand that success is a result of making good decisions, and decisions always involve risk. Therefore, you must learn to take good calculated risks." Then he shared his risk management formula, which I want to share with you, because it is priceless.

Nido said that before you make an important decision, you need to ask yourself four questions:

1. What is the best that can happen if I make this decision?
2. What is the worst that can happen if I make this decision?
3. What is most likely to happen if I make this decision?

4. Am I willing to live with the worst to get to the best?

When you answer these four questions, then you will get a very clear answer as to how you should proceed. When you get confirmation to the questions, then that is a good calculated risk, and you should move on it. If the answers are negative, then you should walk away without regret.

I realized as I read through the questions that they really are the definitive questions when you are faced with difficult choices. Thinking back to my decision to leave my job and start my speaking business 20 years ago, though I didn't know these four specific questions, I instinctively went through the same process.

I was working in a job that I could not stand (and statistics show that I was part of the majority; some studies show as high as 87 percent of people in America get up and go to jobs that they really don't like). I was faced with the decision to stay in that job and have security, or leave the job and live my dreams. I thought about what was the best that could happen if I left my job. I realized that my dream was to make a difference in people's lives and in the process have some financial success and get to travel around the world. I then thought about the consequences and realized that the worst that could happen was to fail and possibly lose my house. Let it be noted that I realize losing my house is a pretty bad consequence, but I wouldn't have died if it had happened. And since I knew I wouldn't die, I believed I could make a comeback! I realized that I would have to struggle, and that this quest would not be easy. I would probably have to work harder than I had ever worked before. But as I looked at the scenario, it came down to a simple mind-set: I was willing to fail at something that I loved rather than succeed at something that I hated.

Since I made that decision, 20 years have come and gone, and I am so happy I made those tough choices. I encourage you to use this formula so you can live your dreams and have greater personal and professional success. Just try it . . . it could change your life!

Speak Positivity, Speak Good into Your Finances

I believe you must speak positivity, speak good into your life and your situation, even when things are not going well. I make a point to tell people to watch their language, because your language has an impact on your mind-set and on the way you will respond to your situation. For instance, never say, "I am poor." Instead, say, "I am wealthy; I do occasionally have some cash flow challenges, but they are always temporary!" Remember that whatever you speak is what you attract, so speak in a positive manner and goodness will flow into your life! I love visiting Australia, and one of the things I love most is when my Aussie friends say "Good on you, mate!" What a great greeting. I have learned to say "Good on you" to my friends, as well as to myself and my finances. Speak goodness into your life and your finances.

Success results for those who are willing to shift their thinking and look at life in its totality and not in segments. To shift from looking at life from a negative perspective to looking at life from a positive perspective, you must act on the new way of thinking. It is not easy to make the shift, but if you are willing to grow your thinking, grow yourself, and take action, then you can start to live life at another level. You must make that choice. You cannot always choose what happens to you, but you can always choose what happens *in* you! You cannot change the circumstances that life throws at you, but you can choose how you respond to the circumstances. My friend Tim Storey, who is a powerful evangelist and motivational speaker, says, "Challenge is a part of life. Your choices do not usually create your challenges, but your choices can always get you out of your challenges!"

Many people say that they took a specific action because they had "no choice." They might say," I gave up on my dreams or my goals because I had no other choice." I agree that although they might not have had a *pleasant* choice, they always have a choice. Will be it be easy? *No!* But is it worth it? The answer is a resounding *yes!* Just keep moving and keep growing and keep believing, and you will find, as I have, that the best is yet to come! Even in the midst of tough times, you can turn your setbacks into greenbacks.

Why Don't You Say *Yes?*

I say that we must overcome our fears and learn to say *yes* to life and to success! Say *yes* to our dreams and *yes* to the life we have always wanted to live. Say *yes* to the possibilities and *yes* to the opportunities that are all around us. You might ask, "What possibilities?" I say that there are possibilities all around you, and if you only stop saying *no*, you will start to see that they are everywhere, especially in the United States. This is the land of possibilities; even in the midst of a recession, there are opportunities. Have you noticed that people are still trying to immigrate to the United States? Have you noticed that people who come to America from other countries seem to do well in

America? In fact, people from other countries become millionaires in America five times faster than people who were born here. Why? Because they might have come from a country where the average wage was $10 a day, and in America they can make $10 an hour. They come with a different perspective and a different mind-set, and they come to America and say *yes* to success. They see money in places that people who were born in America overlook.

I recently had a conversation with friend Peter Tabibian, the owner of a new hamburger chain called Z-Burger. I met Peter at a 7-Eleven store where I often stop for coffee. He had seen me on television, and we talked about his life and his business. He said he came to America as a young man and has always been amazed by this country. He feels that the United States is the greatest country in the world because of the opportunities it offers. I asked him what impact the economy was having on his business, and he said that business was booming. He did say that it was harder than before, but not even close to as hard as it had been when he was growing up in his native land. He said that even in hard times, this was a great time and great place to do business. In fact, I came home from a trip a few weeks ago and turned on the evening news, and there was Peter with former President Bill Clinton, who had visited his restaurant to get some hamburgers. I encourage you to get a *yes* attitude to life and to your dreams. The possibilities are all around for those who are willing to open their eyes and their minds.

This reminds me of the biblical story about the prophet Elisha and his servant Gehazi (2 Kings 6). The prophet Elisha kept forecasting the moves of the enemy and sharing this information with the generals of the army of Israel, who were then able to escape the enemies' traps. The enemy generals got so upset that they asked who the traitor in their ranks was. They were told that there was not a traitor, but rather that the prophet Elisha was telling the army of Israel what was happening. The generals sent troops to the place where Elisha was staying, and when his servant Gehazi awoke, he was stunned to find they had been surrounded by enemy soldiers. Gehazi ran to wake up Elisha and asked him, "My Master, what shall we do?"

Elisha told him, "Do not worry! For those who are with us are greater than those who are with them!" I can see Gehazi now, looking at all the great numbers of enemy soldiers, and then counting on his fingers: "one, two" against the multitude of the enemy. But Elisha prayed and asked God to open Gehazi's eyes. And when his eyes were opened, Gehazi was able to see that the mountains were filled with horses and chariots of fire sent from the Lord!

I pray that you will say *yes* to success and *yes* to the possibilities and that your eyes will be opened to all the incredible opportunities around you. Open your eyes and then move on those goals and dreams, and make them into realities.

Are You Still Waiting for Your Ship to Come In?

Many people speak about how they are waiting for their ship to come in. They patiently sit and wait for their break. I remember my days as a nightclub performer (before the days of *American Idol*), when I was always waiting for my "big break," waiting to be discovered. (I didn't realize then that most of the people in the nightclub were too drunk to discover their way out the front door.) I had always heard people say, "Just keep singing, sing real hard, and one day somebody will give you a break!" I kept waiting for my break, but it never came. Then I learned to stop waiting for my break and start making my breaks. I learned that success is a choice that you must make happen, not a chance that you sit and wait for. I love the old Chinese proverb that states, "He who waits for roasted duck to fly into his mouth waits a long, long time!"

I learned that the best way to grow your future is to first grow yourself. I started a program of self-development, and I decided that I was no longer going to wait for my breaks. I was going to make my breaks. I had a choice: I could continue to wait for my ship to come in or I could swim out to it. I decided to swim, and I am so glad I did, because some of my old friends are still standing at the pier, waiting. Success is not a thing to wait for; it is a thing to be achieved! Make a commitment to be proactive about your success. Make a commitment to take action *today* on your dreams and goals. Make a commitment to read and listen to something positive and uplifting each and every day. (If you don't have a copy of my new *Money Making Music and Motivation,* I highly recommend you get a copy, because it works!) Get started today!

One more secret that I want to share for growing wealth concerns the power of negotiating. When you become a better negotiator, you can improve your bottom line, because at the end of the day, it is not always how much you make but how much you keep. Michael Soon Lee, the author of *Black Belt Negotiating,* was a guest on my radio show and shared a powerful strategy for improving your net worth: learn how to negotiate better, so you can keep more of what you make. Lee says that Americans do not negotiate anything but car prices and home prices, but people from many other countries negotiate everything. He says that almost everything is negotiable if the circumstances are right. Either you can get a better price, or you can get more for your money. In his book, Michael shares some great tips on the power of negotiating to improve your bottom line. First, get over your fear and trepidation about asking for a better price. If you do not ask for the discount, the answer is always "no!" Second, look at the negotiation from the vantage point of the other person. If you can, help them see how making a deal with you can help them grow their business. Third, do your homework on the other person. Fourth, once you make up your mind to negotiate, do not look only at getting a lower price, but also at other options, such as getting something else thrown in, or getting better payment terms. Maybe you can pay over time and get it for low (or no) interest. Every penny you can save adds to your bottom line. Some people will feel that asking for a better price is a hassle, but if you save a few dollars here and a few dollars there, after a year you can have a lot of dollars in your pocket! Get started today!

STEP 6

Be Creative

The next step to turning setbacks into green-backs is to be creative! Think up new ideas and then act on those new ideas! I want to make sure you don't miss the key words in the preceding sentence: *think* and *act.* To turn your situation around, you must *think* and then *act.* To be creative takes a commitment to thoughtful action. You need to think about new ideas and new perspectives and then develop a plan to make those thoughts into realities.

I have heard the saying for years that when you need more money, it is not really a money problem but rather an idea problem. You must work on being more creative in turning your setbacks into greenbacks.

The Creative Shoeshine Man

In my book, *It Only Takes a Minute to Change Your Life!*, I share a story that shows the power of being creative. There was a shoeshine man in a small rural town who was very good at what he did. He wanted to expand and grow his business, so he decided to go to New York City and set up shop. The people in his small town told him that he would never make it in New York City, but he had faith and left to go build his business. When he got to New York, he realized that the competition was fierce; there were shoeshine stands on just about every corner, but he was not deterred. He set up his stand and started looking to grow his business, but it was slow going because of the tremendous amount of competition.

One day, a busy executive left his office a few blocks from the stand of this young shoeshine man. As the executive walked in the direction of the young shoeshine man, he was approached by another shoeshine man who said, "Hey, let me shine your shoes; I need to pay my rent!" The business executive said, "No thanks!"

He went a little further, and another shoeshine man said, "Hey, why don't you stop here and let me shine your shoes—I need the work!" Again, the man said "No thanks!" He went by a third shoeshine man, then a fourth, a fifth, and a sixth before he finally approached the stand of our young shoeshine man. As he approached, the young man was counting: " . . . 97, 98, 99, 100." The young shoeshine man stopped the busy exec and said, "Excuse me, sir, you are the one hundredth person to pass my stand. Today is my birthday, and I am so thankful to have another day to celebrate that I planned to give the one-hundredth person who passed my stand a free

Turn Setbacks into Greenbacks

shoeshine. Please allow me the opportunity to shine your shoes and show my gratitude for having another birthday!"

The busy exec was taken aback and said, "Wow. That is great! I'll take you up on your offer!" He climbed up on the shoeshine stand, and the young man went to work on his shoes. When he finished, the busy exec looked at his shoes; they looked brand new. He said, "This is the best shoeshine I have ever had! Give me a bunch of your business cards; I am going to tell all my friends to come get their shoes shined here!"

The young man gave him a bunch of cards and thanked him for letting him shine his shoes. As the busy exec started to leave for his meeting, he turned around and said, "Hey, it's your birthday. What do you usually charge?"

The young man replied, "Five dollars, sir!"

The busy exec reached into his pocket and pulled out a $100 bill and gave it to the young shoeshine man, saying, "Happy Birthday!" The young man was ecstatic! He then looked to the heavens, then looked at the $100 bill, then looked back to the heavens and said, " . . . 97, 98, 99 . . . "

The lesson here is that you must be creative!

To turn your setbacks into greenbacks, it is critical that you take time to think. You must make it a planned part of your daily routine to simply take time for creative thought. I recommend you

Be Creative

take time every day with a pad and a pencil, or with your computer, and start the thinking session by asking this question, "How can I increase my income today?" I caution you to make sure to have the word *how* at the beginning of that question—don't simply ask, "Can I increase my income today?" If you ask the second question, you are already behind the eight ball, because you are conditioned to think about how bad things are, and your mind will bring up doom and gloom. Don't be plagued by the gloom and doom of the media, and the negative reports about how bad the economy is, how many businesses are failing, and how people are losing their jobs at record numbers. Do not ask the second question; rather, keep your mind and focus on the first question: *"How* can I increase my income today?" If you focus on the *how* question, you will be amazed at the ideas that your mind will generate.

Earl Nightingale made a recording based on *Think and Grow Rich* called *The Strangest Secret*, which became one of the best-selling self-help recordings of all time. It was recorded in the 1950s, but it continues to be a top seller in the self-help industry today. In this recording, Nightingale stated that most people are not successful in life due to the fact that they simply don't think. Those who are willing to think differently are those who have the greatest success.

The Importance of Imagination

The importance of imagination was impressed on me as a youth when I had the opportunity to meet Muhammad Ali. I was visiting my grandmother in Philadelphia, and my mother got tickets to see Muhammad Ali during the taping of a local television show. I was so excited I didn't know what to do. I couldn't wait until it was time to go to the television studio. We even got front-row seats! The champ arrived and shook everybody's hand in the front row, and I was so excited because I could now go home and tell all my friends that I actually shook hands with Muhammad Ali!

I look back now and realize that shaking his hand was fine, but that would wash off. However, during the interview, he said something that would not wash or wear off. He planted a seed that grew as I grew, and helped to shape my thinking. During the interview, he was asked how he had revolutionized the boxing industry so that people flocked to see his fights. His reply was that imagination was the key to his success. He said, "You see, I learned a long time ago that being good was simply not good enough; you've got to have imagination and you've got to dream." Muhammad Ali developed a personality that people either loved or they hated. Those who loved him came to see him win; those who hated him came to see him lose. Either way, every seat was taken!

I learned something that day that will help me for a lifetime. I learned about the power of dreams. I learned that you've got to have imagination, and that you've got to be creative!

Not long ago, I saw a powerful commercial. It was a commercial that featured a little boy watching an old clip of Muhammad Ali after he had defeated Sonny Liston for the World Championship. The young Ali was shouting, "I shook up the world! I shook up the world!" Then the scene shifted with the same little boy sitting with an elderly Muhammad Ali. He looked the little boy in the eye and said, "Shake up the world! Shake up the world!"

I believe we are living in a time when we can do some incredible things, if we are willing to have some imagination. Now is the time to change our thinking and change our finances and our futures. Now is the time to shake up the world! So go get busy! Shake up the world!

The Power of Your Network in Building Wealth

One of the secrets to success in building your wealth is being open to ideas from others and making a commitment to build a network of people who are big thinkers. It is essential to build your network and be able to listen and learn from others. Henry Ford said, "I don't have to know all the answers. I just need to make sure I am smart enough to surround myself with smart people, and I must make sure I am wise enough to listen and learn from them."

I have learned that it is your network that often determines your net worth! Who are you hanging out with? Who are you talking to and sharing ideas with? Are they the type of people who encourage you, inspire you, and pour positive energy into you? Or do they discourage you, depress you, and sap your energy and your creativity? Who you hang with will be who you will become . . . good or bad. So make a commitment to hang with people who will inspire ideas and encourage your entrepreneurial spirit, because those people will have a major impact on helping you turn your setbacks into greenbacks. Your network will definitely help you grow your net worth. Life is not just about what you know, but is also about who you know, and who knows you! A study in *USA Today* stated that, in tough times, 90 percent of jobs are obtained as the result of personal relationships or personal recommendations. People get jobs by way of the people they know, either directly or as a result of connections with others in their network. I hired my marketing manager because one of my best friends got her resume from his sister-in-law, with a recommendation about her work. He knew I was interviewing people to fill a marketing position, and he sent me the woman's information and told me he had gotten a good recommendation from his sister-in-law. On his recommendation, I interviewed her, and after a terrific interview process, I hired her.

The old saying is that there are only six degrees of separation between any two people in the world, yet I believe in this time of social networking that the separation is even less. The key is that you must develop the relationships and work on the relationships. One of the points I think you should focus on during tough times is stepping up your networking. You must be willing to network and develop relationships with other people. Start working on the relationship before you need it. Author and networking expert Harvey Mackay says, "Dig your well before you are thirsty!" Additionally, I recommend that you make a point of making a deposit in the relationship before you try to make a withdrawal. See what you can do to help others before you go back and seek help.

To turn your setbacks into greenbacks, it is essential that you expand your network and work on creating strategic partners. I encourage you to make a commitment to contact people in your network and look for ways that you can be of help to them (and they can be of help to you). It needs to be a win/win opportunity, because the best strategic alliances benefit both parties.

Don't Just Look for a Job . . . Make a Job!

I recommend that you start thinking like the C.E.O. of Y.O.U., Inc. One of the ways you can do this is with network marketing. Network marketing is when a product is distributed via personal network rather than in stores. The money and effort that would typically go toward advertising the product on television or radio are reinvested in incentives for the people who are doing the selling. And those people make their sales by offering the products to people in their networks and offering people in their networks the opportunity to get involved in the business and sell to their own networks.

Some people have a negative impression of network marketing, yet they do not realize that network marketing has helped lots of people become millionaires. When times are tough and unemployment is high, people are looking for creative ways to make more money, and network marketing offers a low-cost way to start a business enterprise. Some people believe that it is a pyramid scheme or a sophisticated Ponzi scheme.

Well, there have been some bad network marketing companies, just as there have been some bad traditional companies. Yet, the majority of network marketing companies are legitimate and excellent vehicles for creating personal wealth. Donald Trump, Robert Kyiosaki, and many other success coaches recommend network marketing as a terrific way to create wealth, and I am adding my voice to theirs. Over the years, I have had the opportunity to speak for hundreds of network marketing events and have stayed in touch with them, and many have become super success stories. I believe network marketing offers people a tremendous opportunity to become independent business owners and to become wealthy!

Volunteer and Make Your Place

Another way I recommend is to look at volunteering to grow your wealth. It sounds like an oxymoron, but it is not.

I was on a plane and met a young man who told me he was frustrated; he had been sending out resumes and had not had any bites. I told him he might have to try something different: volunteer, and be so excellent that you create an opportunity. I asked him if he had ever heard of Michael Baisden, the syndicated radio show host. He told me he had.

I told him that Michael Baisden once worked for the Chicago Transit Authority. He wanted to be a radio host, but no one would hire him, so he volunteered to work for free to show what he could do. He went on to create the top-rated show in the city. From that beginning, he got a big contract and a national syndication deal. I told the young man that I recommended that he volunteer and be so exceptional that he would create spot for himself.

I even decided to give Baisden's example a try. I wanted to expand my national radio presence, and so volunteered to do Monday morning interviews on radio stations for the Radio One Network. I called radio stations across America every Monday morning, and did it for free. After the first ratings period, we found that the program was getting high ratings, so they offered me a longer segment on their XM station—and they paid me! I have since gone on to create one of the top-rated self-help programs on XM Radio. And it started by being willing to volunteer.

Now let me tell you the rest of the story about the young man I met on the plane. I got a note from that young man I had given that recommendation to, and he said he had decided to volunteer, and the results were fantastic. Not only did he get a job, but it was a job that paid more than the job he previously had. If you cannot get people to pay you, but you believe in yourself and in your dreams, I recommend you volunteer and be excellent. In fact, be incredible! Develop a reputation for excellence, and you most often will create a spot for yourself. You will determine your own destiny! In my program, An Attitude of Excellence, I emphatically state that excellence is always your best job security! Why? Because it is . . . excellence always pays the best dividends over time. Therefore, strive for excellence.

"I've Tried Everything!"

Often I talk to people who are going through challenging times, and they will say to me, "I've tried everything!" I will then ask them, have you tried this? Have your tried that?" Typically they will say "Ah, no I didn't think of that!" I respond by saying, "Well maybe you haven't tried everything!" I recommend you sit down with a piece of paper and a pen and write at the top, "How can I achieve x" (whatever you are trying to accomplish), and then think of everything you can. After you have exhausted your own thinking, I want you to ask some of the people in your network about ideas they might have. (By the way, if they say, "It can't be done," then you need to make it a priority to stop listening to them and start growing your network.) In other words, you must recognize that you may have done all you could think of, but that might not be everything. Keep thinking and keep looking for answers!

The Best Is Yet to Come!

In my book, *An Attitude of Excellence,* I share a story that literally changed my life and helped me get a new outlook on life and success. I was a new speaker and I was struggling with my business. I was struggling to keep the phone on and keep the electric company from turning the lights off. It was tough, and I was hoping that someone would call and book me to speak so I could pay my bills. Finally, I got a call from an organization in Orlando, Florida. They booked me to come and speak for their conference. I was so excited that I was going to make some money that I could hardly contain myself.

I went to Florida and gave the speech, and they gave me a standing ovation. I was on cloud nine! I got my check, and they even enclosed a small bonus for doing a good job. I got on the plane to go back home full of excitement because I had gotten paid. But then I started thinking about all my bills and expenses, and I realized that the money was already accounted for. It was allocated to everyone but me! All of a sudden I got depressed because the money was gone before I got a chance to even deposit it in my account.

As I sat there having a pity party with myself, I started talking to an older gentleman across the aisle. He must have sensed that I was struggling, and during the conversation he asked me a question that would have a profound impact on my life. He said, "Young man, how old do you think I am?"

I looked at him and I said, "Well, I would say you are about 60."

He smiled, took off his glasses, looked me right in the eyes, and said: "Young man, I travel around the country speaking to people about health and wealth, and I do it every day. And I want you to know that I am 88 years old, and my best is yet to come!"

In that moment, everything changed for me! If an 88-year-old man could see that his best days were in front of him and not behind him, what in the world did I have to whine and cry about? If an 88-year-old man could have that kind of optimism, what was keeping me from my success? The answer was that the problem was me. I was waiting for success to come to me rather than going out and creating success for myself. Rather than waiting for people to call me, I needed to call them. Rather than sitting in front of the fireplace shouting, "Give me heat," I needed to put something in the fireplace to create some heat.

As I left the plane that day, I was a new person. I went home with a new attitude and new optimism. I got on the phone and started making sales calls and started to talk to more people about my business, and things started to change. That old gentleman was absolutely right—the best was yet to come!

Many years have gone by since that man spoke those words into my life and encouraged me, and a lot has happened. I have had success as a speaker, success as an author, and success with radio and television, yet I believe that this is just the tip of the iceberg of what is possible. I truly believe the best is yet to come! And I believe that your best is yet to come! The question is, do you believe it?

STEP 7

Be Prayerful

The last step should be the first step, because it is actually the most important step, and that is to be prayerful. I have found that prayer changes things and gives you hope. A study from the American Psychological Association states that people with faith tend to live longer. I am amazed that when I interview people who are in their 90s and 100s and ask them their secret to long life, one of the recommendations is always "Have faith and trust God!" I learned years ago that if you want to know how something is done, go ask someone who has done it and learn from them.

Even though I feel that prayer is the most important step, I purposely put it last, because far too often people misinterpret Scripture and think that if they pray, they don't have to do anything else. They have a theology that believes that they need not do anything but pray, and everything will be okay. Yet Scripture clearly states that faith without work is dead, and if a person does not work, they shall not eat! And it encourages people over and over again to pray and then to get up and get busy. Therefore, I purposely left this as the last step because I want to help people, who are waiting for God to drop help in their lap, to get up and get going to help themselves.

My friend Wally "Famous" Amos told my radio audience, "If you want God to drop something in your lap, it is best to put your lap where God is dropping stuff!" Benjamin Franklin wrote, "God helps those who help themselves." Even though many people think the quote is from Scripture, it is not scriptural, but I certainly believe it has truth. I encourage you to pray and have faith, and to use your faith by acting on it. To turn setbacks into greenbacks, you must pray—then move your feet!

Over the years, I have encouraged my friends and clients to understand the three F's of success, which are Faith, Focus, and Follow-through. You must have faith that you are going to live your dreams and achieve big goals. Faith is the substance of things hoped for and the evidence of things not seen. In other words, faith involves the stuff that comes from having hope and believing that your thoughts and dreams can come true. It is walking and moving forward with the confidence of positive expectations—faith to expect good things to come from your actions and to see things in your mind that are not yet a reality as possible. My friend Dale Smith Thomas told my radio audience that F.A.I.T.H. is the opposite of F.E.A.R. Fear is False Evidence Appearing Real, while Faith is Finding Answers In The Heart! God asks us to have faith, and if we would just have the sincere faith of a mustard seed, we would be able to move mountains! If you are going to do incredible things with your life and have massive success, it is going to take faith!

Next you must have Focus. Success is not about hocus pocus, but rather about focus! You must focus on your dreams and goals and not be distracted by all the noise and static that is constantly trying to take us off course and off target. That is why I have been shouting over and over again about the importance of goals and why you must take time to think about them, write them down, and then read them regularly! From the moment most people get up until the moment they go to sleep, they are being bombarded by a constant barrage of advertisements and messages from others that can take their focus away from their goals and dreams. It is like the siren song that will pull us off course. Sometimes you have to stop and turn off the world and focus for a moment on your dreams and goals and what it will take to achieve those goals.

Next is Follow-through, which is the step that involves actively going through the business development process. I say that you must go through the process, because it is a part of the circle of life that you have a beginning, a middle, and an ending of all actions. I learned years ago when I

Be Prayerful

started playing tennis that you must start with setting up for the swing, then you must swing and hit the ball, then you must follow through. If I didn't complete one of those first two steps, I would not get the shot across the net, and when I didn't finish the shot with a follow-through, the shot was weak and ineffective. Then, years later, I started playing golf and the instructor said the same thing: start by setting up, then swing the club and hit the ball, and then follow through. One day at a tournament, I forgot to follow through, and all my shots were going all over the place. A friend stopped and looked at my swing and said, "Willie you are not completely following through on your shots!" I stopped and thought about it, and realized he was right. So I tried again with a full follow through, and the results were dramatically different. I was back in the game, because I was willing to follow through on what I had started.

I have found the same thing to be true in the success process. You must set up and prepare for the necessary actions that will get you moving in the direction of your goal. Then you must take action—committed, consistent action. Then you must follow through and finish what you start. Follow through on the items you said you would follow through on, because your word must always be your bond, and if you say it, then you must do it! You must follow through on your calls and e-mails and business communications. The wealth-iest people I know always find a way to follow through and communicate with people who want to do business with them. You must follow through on the items you have written down on your lists, and the steps to success you have developed.

After you do the three F's for Financial Success, I want you to add the three P's to Prosperity, which are to Pray, Plan, and Pursue! First you should be humble enough to take time to pray, because prayer changes things. Prayer leads to hope, and you need hope to succeed, especially in challenging times. Scripture says, "We know that tribulation produces perseverance, and persever-ance, character and character, hope!" You must have hope, and prayer will lead to hope! Don't be too proud to pray because prayer can empower and strengthen you for the journey. Bruce Wilkin-son wrote a book some years ago called *The Prayer of Jabez*. It shared the story of a man named Jabez who prayed that God would enlarge his territory, and God granted him what he requested! Why? Because Jabez was willing to trust God and pray for greater prosperity! Pray for what you want and be willing to ask God to bless you, and remember it is God who gives you the power to get wealth, yet it is up to us to be good stewards and to use our blessing to establish His covenant, and to help others. First Pray! Remember prayer

153

gives you hope and the power to keep going, in spite of the challenges.

Speaker John Alston shared a story with me about the impact of hope. He said that a science club placed four frogs in a vat of water. They kept the frogs in that vat of water until they were almost out of air, and at the last moment they pulled the frogs out. The next day, they put those same four frogs in a vat of water, and they put four new frogs in a separate vat of water. They kept all the frogs under water until they were almost out of air, and then held them an additional 15 seconds. The new frogs, which had not been through the previous experience, gave up and died; but the four frogs from the day before held on and lived. The old frogs had hope and optimism and a belief that they would get through the challenge, because they had been through the earlier experience.

Next you must plan! Plan your work, and work your plan! If you want to create wealth, it is critical that you plan. Your plan can be fluid and flexible, but you need to have a business plan and an action plan. No great building was ever built without a blueprint, and no great army wins without a battle plan. You too should have a plan. You might have to make adjustments and changes as you go along, but at least you will know where you are going. Along with planning, you must position yourself so you are ready when the economy comes back.

Wayne Gretsky said that the key to massive success was always positioning. He said, "A good hockey player plays where the puck is. A great hockey player plays where the puck is going to be!" Successful people position themselves where the money is going to be, not where it is now. Get in position now for the comeback!

Finally you must pursue, to go after it with all your might! Most people are waiting for their ships to come in, but the wise ones are swimming out to their ships. I will say this over and over and over again: First you must pray, and then you must get up and go to work. When you get red hot on your goal and pursue it, I believe you will find that things will start to happen that you could not imagine. If you want wealth in your life, you need to make the commitment to pursue. Pray, and then move your feet.

Are You the One to Overcome These Tough Times?

In my twelfth-grade year, I had an experience that changed my life and gave me a new perspective. I had not been serious about my school work and was not pursuing excellence and was just getting by. One day, while I was in homeroom, there was an announcement on the public address system that said, "We have a motivational speaker who will be giving a presentation this morning, and everyone must attend!"

I told my teacher, "I don't need to hear a motivational speaker. I want to stay here in homeroom and do my homework—it's only two weeks late!"

She said, "Young man, you really need some motivation!"

I didn't want to go to the assembly that day, but I went because it was mandatory. I went to the auditorium and sat in the back row and threw my hood over my head and decided I was not going to listen. Yet, somewhere in his message, the speaker got my attention. He said, "Someone in this room has something special inside of them. Someone in this room is going to do great things with his or her life. I don't know which one it is, but I know for sure that it is one of you!"

In that moment, something woke up on the inside of me, and I heard a voice saying, "It's me! I'm the one!"

When the speaker finished, he walked off the stage and walked up the center aisle. He went right toward my row, and I ran to the edge of the row and said, "Excuse me, sir!" He stopped, and looked me in my eye, and I wanted to tell him that I was the one he was talking about, but the words would not come out. I tried and I tried, but the words would not come out! Finally he nodded

Turn Setbacks into Greenbacks

his head and told me to have a good day. As he walked away, I was so upset because I couldn't get the words out. At the same time, I was excited because something inside me had changed.

Years went by. While making a transfer in the Denver airport, I was walking from one gate to another, when all of a sudden, I saw that man! I hadn't seen him since high school. I got weak in the knees, but I pulled myself together and walked over to him. I said, "Excuse me, sir. I am sorry to disturb you, but my name is Willie Jolley and I need to ask you a question."

He said, "Are you Willie Jolley, the author and speaker? I have seen you on television, and I have read your books."

I said, "Thank you, sir, but that is not why I stopped you. I need to ask you a question. Did you come to Roosevelt Senior High in Washington, D.C. in the mid-1970s and speak to the students?"

He said, "Yes, I did."

I asked, "Do you remember telling the students that someone in the room had something special in them?"

Again he responded, "Yes, I do remember."

I then said, "Sir, I couldn't tell you then, but I can tell you now . . . it was me! I was the one you were talking about!"

I have found, as I travel around the world, that many times, when I am speaking to students, I get

157

Be Prayerful

a sense that someone in that room has something special. Someone in that room has an unique reason for being here. That person is supposed to do something great with his or her life. I don't know who it is, but I do know it is someone in that room.

Today, I decided to write this piece because I have a sense that someone reading this book has something special inside of them. I believe you picked up this book and came this way because you are supposed to do something incredible with your life. I don't know which person it is, but I believe it is one of you! Are you the one?

IT'S BY YOUR FAITH"

Willie Jolley and Brian Taylor

Spoken Word:
Now as I read the scriptures
More and more I found this promise of power
That was given to us if we would just have faith
The more I read, the more I found
That as you believe, so shall you receive
Then I learned a little more
It says all things are possible
If you can just believe
Then it said if a man believeth in the heart
So as he is
And I read a little more
It said you achieve not because of your unbelief

Wow and then we found we could have
Mountain moving faith
We could change our circumstances
Change our lives by the power of our faith
It said for assuredly if you have the faith of a
    mustard seed
You will say to this mountain move from here to
    there
And it will move and nothing will be impossible to
    you
I said Uh Oh I'm on to something here
It said whosoever (and I thought I was a who-so-
    ever)
It said whosoever says unto this mountain be
    removed
And be ye cast into the sea and does not doubt in
    his heart
But believes that those things he says will come to
    pass
He will have whatever he says
Or if you have the faith of a mustard seed
You can say to the mulberry tree be pulled up by
    the roots
And it be planted in the sea, and it will obey you
Oh I thought I was onto something then
And I said okay what else can I learn
And it said ask and you shall receive
Seek and ye shall find
Knock and the door will be opened unto you
For everyone who asks receives, and everyone
    who seeks finds
And everyone who knocks the door will be opened
Unto them

159

Be Prayerful

Therefore most people receive not because
they either ask not, they seek not, or they knock
   not
And then they wonder why not!
You must have faith. It's as simple as that
Folks you got to have faith
You got to walk by faith
Talk by faith
Live by faith
Move by faith
Oh, act on your faith
You got to go out and understand that you can
   move mountains
You can achieve incredible things
If you're willing to step out on your faith
Keep it!
Keep the Faith!

© 2004 Seakara Music (ASCAP)/Willie Jolley Music (BMI)

Conclusion

In life, there will be setbacks, downturns, and challenges—not maybe, not might, but definite setbacks and problems. Yet it is important to remember that this is not personal, and it is not permanent. This too shall pass! Everyone feels the pinch of an economic downturn; it is an equal opportunity pain. Yet in every burden there is a blessing, and if we are wise, it is out of these challenges that we can grow our wealth and success. Recession and depressions always lead to progressions. History has shown that out of each severe economic downturn, we became stronger as a country and our economy expands. After each economic downturn, we see greater increase in the general standard of living, and more people learn about wealth building and join the ranks of the millionaires. The key is that when you are at the bottom, it is critical that you do not give up hope but maintain a positive mind-set. If you are willing to think about possibilities and if you stay positive, even in the midst of extreme challenges, you will realize that you can turn this around, and you can be the victor and need not be the victim! It is in these moments of challenge that we will either move forward toward our goals and dreams or we will fall back towards our fears. The choice is up to you!

So I close this book with this thought: Whatever you do, hold on to your dreams. This is not the time to give up and throw in the towel! This is not the time to quit! Tough times do not last, but tough people do! You must not just go through these tough times. You must grow through these tough times!

We stand at a time when it is up to us to make the most of this moment and to take advantage of the opportunities that are all around. Yet, wherever there are opportunities, there will also be challenges, and I pray that we will not only be fit and able to meet those challenges but to conquer those challenges and move to greater levels of success. I wish that you grow and stretch this year beyond what you thought you could do!

So I implore you to think big and make a commitment to focus on the positive and not all the negative gloom and doom. I believe that the best way to predict the future is to create the future, and so I believe this is going to be an incredible year! So get up, get dreaming, get going, get stretching, and get to really living life at another level! I pray that you work hard, work smart, and trust God! And finally, I pray that you prosper and be in good health, as your soul prospers! Remember, you very well are The One! Live Your Dreams . . . and know that Your Best Is Yet to Come! God Bless You!

About the Author

Willie Jolley is truly a renaissance man! He is an award winning speaker and singer, a best-selling author, and a popular radio and television personality. He is the CEO of Willie Jolley Worldwide, a professional development organization that focuses on developing excellence in corporate and individual performance. He is also the chairman of the board of the non-profit ministry organization, Jolley Good News. In 1999, Willie Jolley was named "One of the Outstanding Five Speakers in the World" by Toastmasters International, and in 2005, he was inducted into The Speakers Hall of Fame. He is a five-time Washington area (WAMMIE) award-winning singer. His television broadcasts are seen on PBS and CBS Television, and his radio broadcasts are heard on weekends on XM Radio and daily on numerous stations across the country.

He is the author of two international best-selling books: *It Only Takes a Minute to Change Your Life* and *A Setback Is a Setup for a Comeback.*

And his latest book, *An Attitude of Excellence*, has become a national phenomenon. His new "Willie Jolley" music is now the number one downloaded motivational music on the Apple Itunes site.

Willie Jolley regularly speaks for top corporations and organizations in the United States. His clients include Wal-Mart, Dell, Ford, Verizon, Marriott, DuPont, Nabisco, Chevron, Dominos Pizza, Amway, McDonald's, Chase Manhattan, Allstate Insurance, Pepsi, Coca-Cola, Sprint, Borders Books, Prudential of Australia, The American Society of Association Executives, and the US Army, Navy, and Marines. In addition, his program for youth, Dare 2 Dream, is one of the top-selling youth videos in the United States. Willie Jolley is a graduate of The American University and Wesley Theological Seminary. His mission in life is to help people maximize their God-given talents and abilities so they can do more, be more, and achieve more! He lives in Washington, DC with his wife and son.

Willie Jolley
Success Products

Business-Building Products
- Double Your Business (Live in Australia): DVD
- Attitude of Excellence: Leadership Development DVD
- The Will to Win: 6 DVDs
- T.I.P.S. for Speaking Success: DVDs & CDs
- The Entrepreneur's Rich Success Treasure Chest: DVDs & CDs
- Willie Jolley XM Radio Interviews Collection

Motivational/ Inspirational Products
- Money Making Music & Motivation: DVD & CDs
- A Setback Is a Setup for a Comeback: DVD or CDs
- It Only Takes a Minute to Change Your Life: CDs
- The Willie Jolley Jazz/Gospel Combo: CDs
- Dare 2 Dream: Youth Motivational DVD Pack
- Willie Jolley Winners Wake-up Call

Preview or Purchase
These Products & More at:
www.williejolley.com